# A FLAG AT THE POLE

# A FLAG

# AT THE POLE

## THREE SOLILOQUIES

## PAXTON DAVIS

### ETCHINGS BY HAROLD LITTLE

ATHENEUM   *New York*   1976

LIBRARY OF CONGRESS CATALOGING IN PUBLICATION DATA


Davis, Paxton. A flag at the pole.

SUMMARY: *A fictional account told in the first person by Ernest Shackleton, Robert Scott, and Roald Amundsen of the motives that drove them and the physical and psychological difficulties they encountered in their attempts to be "first at the South Pole."*

1. Shackleton, Sir Ernest Henry, 1874–1922—Juvenile fiction. 2. Scott, Robert Falcon, 1868–1912—Juvenile fiction. 3. Amundsen, Roald Engelbregt Gravning, 1872–1928—Juvenile fiction. [1. Shackleton, Sir Ernest Henry, 1874–1922—Fiction. 2. Scott, Robert Falcon, 1868–1912—Fiction. 3. Amundsen, Roald Engelbregt Gravning, 1872–1928—Fiction. 4. Explorers—Fiction]
I. Little, Harold II. Title.
PZ7.D2975Te [Fic] 76–81
ISBN 0–689–30522–2

*for Peggy with love*

*The* conquest of the South Pole in the first decade of the twentieth century was the climactic episode in the great adventure of heroic exploration initiated in 1775 by Captain Cook's circumnavigation of Antarctica. English, Russian, French, American, Belgian, German, Norwegian, Scot and Swedish sailors and scientists by their labors led the way; but in the end the Pole itself came down to three extraordinary men, one Anglo-Irish, one Norse and one English. Their names were Ernest Shackleton, Roald Amundsen and Robert Falcon Scott; and their courage, dedication and magnanimity, representative of the best of an age still unashamed to value such virtues, dramatically demonstrate the truth Nansen spoke when he said that in polar exploration "it is the man *that matters.*"

# CONTENTS

SHACKLETON 1909       3

AMUNDSEN 1911     43

SCOTT 1912       81

# A FLAG AT THE POLE

# SHACKLETON

## 1909

AH, BUT A MAN'S REACH . . .

Old Browning, of course; and right too. It's the struggle that counts. Winning is wonderful, and one should if one can, but it's trying and trying that makes for the fun, it's zest for the contest that sets off a man— against the wind and the water, the ice and the snow, against darkness and ignorance, weakness and sloth, against one's own self . . . Sometimes I even think in his meters.

But he saw how it goes, Bob Browning did, knew how a life went, his own perhaps, mine certainly—knew how a man might spend his days and nights and weeks and months and finally spend the fruits and substance of his years pursuing what luck or chance or fate or God might nonetheless deny him; knew, and knew how to say, that even so, it's aspiration and effort that bring the real satisfaction, not achievement itself. A comfort, that; for I've tried and I've failed, not once but twice, at the big thing, the biggest—

And both times turned back. . . .

The Pole. The South Pole. It was the summit of my dreams, the mountain, so to say, to scale which I'd've sacrificed everything, for England, for Emily, for myself. Well, but then, bless Bob, "what does the mountain care?"

The world is large and various. Globes and charts hardly hint at the scale of its amplitude, and only he who sees it for himself, as I have, can fully catch the compass of its incredible multiplicity—the enormous blue bowl of the sky above, the wild swirl of its waters, the spill of its colors, the fall of the light. Once, becalmed off Batavia, I watched the morning fishermen scuttle out to sea while behind them the sun rose upon such a glory I halfway thought I heard the music of the spheres. As for the aurora of Antarctica. . . .

I've been a lucky man, all told. Every boy dreams of the world and what he'll make of it, spins visions of such deeds and conquests as bring the heart to a gallop, but unlike most, whose years see it all ravel out in routine, I've lived to live my dreams alive, seen them swell and grow and take flesh and shape and motion and direction; and if I've failed a time or two—why, I'm young yet, another day's coming, and with it another chance to pit my wit and my will against the dark unknown.

The Irish in me, I suppose, that optimism; for a bit of Ireland runs in my blood, after all, though my good Yorkshire kinsmen blush to the claim. My dear mother was Irish, for a fact, as robust and tenacious of spirit as the long lineage of County Cork could boast, and Irish lay behind my English father too; while I myself was born in County Kildare, seat of poets and dreamers and men of good cheer since the world began. Let who will laugh at my pride; we're a fighting Irish breed, we Shackletons, and the devil befall him who thinks otherwise. As our motto conveys, *Fortitudine Vincimus*— "By endurance we conquer."

Appropriate too, considering how things've gone; for what with this and that, I've had my ups and downs, as what Irishman worth his glass has not; and it tells the tale of my Antarctic adventures in a nutshell. I need and seek no pity, though, for unlike my colleague and rival, Captain Scott, who for all his beauty of spirit and glamour of accomplishment must spend his life a prisoner of melancholy, I've had the best the world offers all along, a big affectionate family, a happy childhood, good times, good luck, a wealth of friends and a love old Browning himself might envy; and still do and expect to, thanks. My happy Irish heart's been a blessing that's seen me through one misadventure after another, and I'm grateful for it.

I'm grateful also that I found my niche, as they say, early on, even if I found it quite by chance. For the descendant of Quakers, I was a carefree but aimless boy, interested in everything but focussed on nothing, and my schoolwork, apart from my love of poetry and my knack for memorizing it by the yard, was indifferent; and, with no yen for university, I was willing enough when my father, himself a schoolmaster though by then a physician too, suggested I try the sea. I'd grown up on Marryat and Henty, knew the exploits of Drake and Hawkins and Raleigh as well as I knew Tennyson, and for Verne's Captain Nemo I felt a fascination, bordering on mania, that persists to this day; sailing was ripe in my imagination. It meant an apprenticeship and hard work, but I scarcely minded that, being quick to learn when I chose to, and afterward . . . well, afterward I could picture myself foursquare against the mast, a swaggering salt who'd seen the world and its wonders, a bit of a buccaneer, a darling of destiny—Nemo, in short.

So I shipped out most cheerfully, and though our meagre means put a berth in the Royal Navy beyond my grasp, I was as well satisfied to take papers with the Merchant Marine, which for its part seemed equally pleased to have on its rolls a strapping sixteen-year-old with an eye for sail and a weakness for Browning; and by the time I was twenty-two I'd done it all, seen it all and worked my way up the ladder, touched and tasted Chile and India, America and China, the Indies and Japan, rounded both great Capes, loaded and unloaded every cargo imaginable—rice and hemp, bananas and

coal and indigo—come down with and recovered from
seasickness, fever and lumbago (and a hangover once
or twice, truth to tell), mastered sail and then steam,
studied engines and charts, learned astronomy and navigation, memorized most of *Paracelsus* and all of *Prospice*
and passed my test for First Mate. Busy? A bit; but not
a bad show for a lad of faint promise.

I loved it too, abaft and forward, above decks and below, loved the swell and the spray, the steamy tropic
nights and the rich aromas of the East, the jabber of the
Wogs and the chatter of my companions, and I suppose I might've kept at it forever, eventually, if my
strength kept and my luck held, with a ship of my own;
but I was too restless to settle for security. Though my
prospects were rosy, my interests were widening; I had a
taste for adventure, a hankering for fame and by then a
curiosity that embraced the world, and my membership
in the Royal Geographical Society, which elected me
Fellow, only whetted them all; and when in 1900 talk
grew of a big expedition to look out Antarctica, I saw
where my future lay.

Terra Australis, Terra Incognita—so seamen of old
in awe and wonder called it . . . But I knew nothing of
the place, beyond what legend held and hearsay colored,
for it was the last great unknown the globe's surface
boasted, scarcely glimpsed, still uncharted, its size and
shape and even whether it was land or ice or something
of both all matters of babble and blather and fanciful
guesswork; but there too lay its appeal for a lad of my

stripe, the challenge, the dare, for it offered by some happy harmony the opportunity to do what no man had done before me, the chance to pit myself against who could foresee what hazards, the privilege of bringing a smack of the knowledge of science to what till then had been only ignorance and silence. All of them worked on my imagination and deepened the draw, as did the notion of a rousing British triumph at the Pole; but there was more to it yet, something that spoke to me personally, privately, something formless but beckoning I couldn't put a name to—the prospect of struggle perhaps, the pull of the dark, high drama, romance; in each I heard the "lure of little voices," and when the call came for volunteers, I was there with the first.

It took a bit of doing, though, for I was far from alone in feeling the fascination of Antarctica; and moreover, as I promptly discovered, the expedition was to be a Navy show in and out, led and staffed by regulars and aimed at burnishing the Admiralty's prestige. I counted myself as good a sailor as any, for a fact, and tipped my cap to no man; but as a mercantile officer, I was outside the club and thus well below the salt; and it was only thanks to the intervention of Sir Clements Markham, who swung a lieutenancy for me in the Royal Naval Reserve, that a way was found to secure me the berth to which I was immodest enough to believe my talents and experience entitled me. Later he turned on me, Markham did, but that's another story.

It was his expedition, right enough, the dream he'd

nurtured and struggled to realize for most of his life; and so, I soon saw, was its leader, Commander Robert Falcon Scott, whom in fact I was to serve as third lieutenant. Markham had spotted him years before and shepherded him along ever since, overseen his progress in the Navy, and based the expedition he was too old to lead himself on the employment of Scott as his surrogate; and by the time I entered the picture, Scott was little less than Markham's pet, the very model of a proper English sea captain—gentleman's bearing, good public-school accent, a stickler for Navy discipline and etiquette, reserved manner, all that. I'm not one to seek enemies and I hope in the long haul I've created none of Scott, but I knew straightaway we weren't made to hit it off. Blame my natural exuberance, blame my years in the easy democracy of the merchant fleet: I was as much at home with the swabbies below deck as I was with the toffs above, the Navy officers with whom alone I was supposed, as they say, to fraternize, and though Scott was too courteous to reveal his disapproval directly I could tell from the way his eyes narrowed and his lips pursed he didn't care for my breezy Irish style. . . . Remarkable eyes, those, unforgettable eyes, a deep blue that could recede to a piercing violet; they'd've curdled the marrow of a rhinoceros.

He was a first-class commander, though, make no mistake, for though Markham might pet him, Markham had clearly picked the right man to pet. He had an eye for everything and a beautifully organized mind that sorted and stored all he saw and heard with incredible precision, and his leadership, prim and aloof though I thought it, was firm and fair and expressed in a fashion that showed he had a genuine grasp of the capacities of his staff and the complexities of our task. It was what lay behind and beneath that frosty formality—snobbishness? indifference? melancholy?—that ruffled my wings and defied my understanding; and does yet.

Still, I meant him no ill nor he me, and with the rest of the staff and crew I quickly found myself on good and easy terms, outsider though for a time Scott had made me feel I was. My background in sail fitted me handsomely for the *Discovery,* a trim ship of oak and elm especially built to ride out and crush the ice the expedition would encounter in southern waters, and it gave me the cachet I needed with the regulars, such fellows as Royds and Skelton, who once they realized I knew the knots as well as they—and perhaps, when it came to sail, a bit better—forgot their prejudices and accepted me as one of their own. There was much to do, in any case, chores of so many kinds outside the routine run of an ordinary ship that no sensible man could've stood on the rigidities of Navy ceremony, and being naturally of an energetic and bustling cast I took on whatever came, catering, ship's stores, entertainment, the expedition magazine, much else. Besides, my irregular position was not as unusual as I'd at first believed. Armitage, for one, was a veteran of the Merchant Marine too, while most of the scientists were plain, unapologetic civilians, even farther outside the charmed circle than we. I found them immensely congenial, broad and varied in their interests and ready at any time to show me this or that about which I'd previously known nothing. Mill and Koettlitz and Ferrar and Bernacchi were always up for a smoke and a jaw, and with one of the technical staff in particular I established a friendship as warm as the luckiest man could boast.

It's one of those paradoxes Bob Browning himself might've cherished that my friend became Scott's closest friend too, and is still; but Bill Wilson made the gift of his affection no man's exclusive possession, being far too large of heart and mind for rivalry, either for his own sake or as a confederate or participant in the rivalries of others. He was a Cambridge man, a physician by calling, but more, much more, a zoologist and ornithologist and artist as well, not to mention the vast general culture he brought to all he did, his knowledge of religion, philosophy and literature. More nights than I can count he'd join me on the bridge to swap Browning and Tennyson, Swinburne and Meredith, Wordsworth and Southey and Cowper and Gray, and I can hardly exaggerate the breadth and depth he added to my own much spottier understanding of their poetry. But to leave it there is only to hint at the richness of his personality. Perhaps because of his long ordeal of grave illness, perhaps simply because it was his nature, of us all he stood farthest above the frictions of daily life— kind, generous, unruffled, imperturbable, free of pettiness, free of mean ambition, the single soul aboard the *Discovery* whose judgment was invariably balanced, humane and disinterested; and though with the rest I could no more be like him than write in alexandrines, I could appreciate the standard his calm superiority set. It may be that Scott and I are the better explorers, but Wilson's incomparably the better man.

It was a busy business, at all events, a matter of getting to know the ship and each other, but we took the voyage out quickly and well; and New Zealand gave us a reception worthy of kings. We berthed there at Lyttelton for more than a month to complete preparations for setting off south, repairing the hull, overhauling the sails, restowing the holds, replacing supplies, and though I found much to do aboard, I had time also for making the rounds, as most did, and was to be glad subsequently I had; for in their enthusiasm for our venture the New Zealanders far outshone our own countrymen, contributing generously to our subsidy and encouraging our spirits with their support; and in a later time, with my own expedition, I was to find crucial backing from amongst the friends I had made there.

Then to their smiles and tears we were off again, entering the ice pack on Christmas Day, and it was shortly after the dawn of the New Year, 1902, that I had my first sight of the land that has compelled my fascination and devoured my energy since. Terra Australis, Terra Incognita . . . It rose from its mists like a phantom from a dream, spectrally white, wreathed in

fog, its sea reaches guarded by jagged outriding icebergs
that clutched the sky before and then above us like
gigantic claws. Scott's plan was to survey such coast as
he could, before winter came on, for the best possible
base; so it was February and we'd passed up Capes Adare
and Wadworth, Wood Bay and Granite Harbor before
we entered McMurdo Sound and settled ourselves at
last in a bay on the south side of Ross Island. There, our
anchored ship serving as shore station, we looked out
onto the Great Ice Barrier, the seemingly endless albinic
plain, as flat as a desert and altogether as featureless,
that was to prove the first mammoth obstacle to our
assault on the Pole.

That was still but the vaguest of dreams, however, no
part of our charter and as yet no more than a possibility
none dared to bespeak, and if it came at all it would
come later, the following summer at the soonest; for the
Antarctic winter now descended with a ferocity that,
though we'd heard the tales, astonished us all, and in
learning to cope with its special hazards and terrors, we
had no choice but to put aside, at least for the moment,
such visions of glory. I was never idle. As storeman and
caterer, I worked with Koettlitz devising menus we
hoped would combat the immemorial curse of scurvy,
creating elaborate variations on the monotonous round
of tinned meat, fruit, vegetables and butter, adding fresh
mutton and seal as often as possible; I took salinities
daily, helped Hodgson with his fish traps, tried to learn
magnetism from Bernacchi, betweentimes edited the

magazine; but my most important task was to learn with the rest what had to be learned if we were to extend our venture beyond the base at Hut Point—how to sledge.

We knew nothing about it beyond what we'd read, and what little we thought we knew proved to be wrong. Nansen, to be sure, had urged Scott to use dogs as he himself had done in the Arctic; but the dogs we'd brought balked, fought, tangled their harness, and when we tried to help by pulling with them they lay down in the snow and refused to pull at all. The sledges were heavier than they looked, and loaded with provisions they resisted everything but the most exhausting efforts to budge them into motion. Worse yet, even when we got them going, were the difficulties of the surface— sastrugi, roughness, hard ice, invisible crevasses—and the fury of the weather, which with its terrifying blizzards and incredible cold drained from even the strongest of us, amongst whom I place myself, all but the last of our energy, vitality and will.

Hard times, hard lines . . . We had much to learn and learned it only slowly. Yet learn what we could we did, ignorance, clumsiness and awful climate notwithstanding; and as the long dark night of winter wore on, we began slowly to master the innumerable skills and disciplines we'd need for the work that awaited when daylight returned. Armitage readied a party to journey westward in search of the South Magnetic Pole. Royds and Koettlitz prepared to sledge with four others for Cape Crozier. I supervised their provisioning and loading,

kept up my salinities and magnetism, wrote miles of
verse for the *South Polar Times* (and signed it
"Nemo"), worked endlessly and fruitlessly with the
dogs, reconnoitered Minna Bluff, pitched a tent in a
blizzard, fought off scurvy; and with Wilson initiated a
program of daily hiking by which we determined to
toughen ourselves for the task Scott informed us we
should undertake that summer. For by now the commitment was firm and all preparations aimed at its accomplishment: we three—Scott, Wilson and I—would
try for the Pole.

The Pole? Ernest Shackleton? . . . Well, sir, I was as
flattered, to crib the old tale, as the whore asked to the
church supper. Oh, to be sure, I told myself I'd earned
the right, by my competence, hard work, sturdy phy-
sique, and willing spirit; but all the same I was *pleased,*
pleased at myself for punching my way past the Navy
toffs, pleased with Scott for recognizing my gifts despite
his personal distaste—and I vowed then and there to
see he'd have no cause to regret it. He'd given me the
chance of my life to make good, while as for the danger
—well, I hadn't come south for a feather bed.

Nor had I come south to be humbled, no more by
Antarctica than by the nobs of the Royal Navy, and
when we set off at last in November it was with the
happiest of hearts, eyes bright, heads high, cheered on
by the men of the *Discovery* as we went whizzing away,
bright sledge flags flying, down the great white sweep of
the Barrier. The dogs ran well, all nineteen of them,

and for a day or two, so smooth was the surface, we three had to run alongside simply to keep up. Above us the sun shone fair. Immense towers of cottony cumuli filled the brilliant blue sky. The air was brisk but almost warm. We joked and shouted and sang as we went, and in the tent at night we read Darwin aloud.

But then, without warning, our luck turned. The sky abruptly darkened. Within a few hours a blizzard had set in, and for a day and then another we were powerless to move. When we got going again new troubles appeared. The dogs slowed. The surface roughened. Our daily mileage fell. Wilson's joints began to ache, then his ankle, and he took a cold. A day later I started coughing myself, a dry, persistent cough that seemed to rip my chest open and robbed me night after night of the sleep I needed and craved; and—though I kept it to myself—my gums were tender. It was the first sign of scurvy.

But Scott seemed sound, while Wilson and I pretended to be, and we managed to move on, past Borchgrevink's Furthest South, past a sextant reading of seventy-nine degrees, and though the dogs looked nearly done our spirits lifted to know we were now beyond the southernmost reach of all efforts before us. For a few days the weather brightened again. My cough lessened. Wilson moved more easily. The temperature rose. Then, as suddenly as before, everything came apart. Snow crystals began to obstruct the surface. The dogs pulled more and more poorly, at last unable to break the loads, and that left us no choice, if we were to continue, but to proceed by relay, dividing the sledges, helping the dogs haul three of them forward and then retracing our steps to repeat the lap with the remaining pair. But the duplication of labor was exhausting and enervating and that, in turn, brought back Wilson's rheumatism and my cough. Instead of advancing our march, the dogs were holding us back, and they continued to weaken, daily, perceptibly, whining and panting at the least exertion.

So, though less dramatically, did we; but we kept at it all the same, and if conditions steadily worsened as December deepened, the scenes through which we moved provided extraordinary—if temporary—compensation. The emptiness and silence were total. I could not have imagined a landscape at once so desolate and beautiful, for the bleak unbroken whiteness of the ice was offset by a constantly shifting stream of color from the mountain range ahead, which even as we watched could change from scarlet to lavender to the ripe purple of plum; while above us the sun shook out the miracle of its aurorae, staining the immense velvet twilight with an endless succession of bows and rings and haloes of inconceivable radiance and variety. They seemed flung like gems across the great carpet of heaven, a vision of such splendor and mystery as even the brush of a Constable or Corot could scarcely have caught. Our awe reduced us to a silence as mute as that of the Barrier; and, as Wilson later put it, if it didn't quite humble me at least it stopped the breezy babble of my tongue.

By then more than wonder at Creation was stilling my talk, however, and slowing me too, for as our relaying continued into a third week and a fourth the symptoms of whatever was plaguing me grew steadily worse; and though I concealed my discomfort as best I could— and perhaps by way of stubborn compensation even increased my share of the sledging—I could no longer hide the seriousness of my cough or the toll it was taking of my strength. All night, sides, chest and gut torn with pain, I wheezed and hacked asthmatically, which robbed not only me but Scott and Wilson of essential sleep; now and then I spat up blood; more mornings than not my gums ran red as well. Yet I was hardly alone in showing the onset of scurvy, for both of the others had begun to run fevers too, to suffer vague aches and swollen joints and complain of tender gums; and to make bad matters worse we were all three continually hungry, full rations notwithstanding. On the march now we talked of nothing but food, of what and where and how much we'd eat on our return; and at night, when we slept at all, we dreamed endlessly of dishes and bowls and tables and trestles piled to overflowing with steaks and roasts and grills, meats broiled and baked, vegetables and fruits and salads and pastries, pies and cakes and turnovers and tarts, dreamed of sauces and dressings and towers of condiments, jams and jellies, marmalades and preserves, honey and pickle and relish and gravies by the gallon. . . . I made list upon list of the dishes I craved, and Wilson screamed in his sleep from a recurrent nightmare of shouting for a waiter who refused to hear or serve him; while Scott, though he claimed to taste as well as see the food he dreamed of, argued finally that the hunger was worse than the work.

The dogs had failed and now we too, if far from failing, had badly faltered. We crossed the eightieth parallel and then the eighty-first, but by mid-month we all knew, though none yet said so openly, that we could hope no longer to make the Pole. Snatcher died, the first of the dogs to go, and the rest seemed about to. Yet somehow, aching, panting, bleeding, silent, we pushed on, hauling dogs as well as sledges; and on Christmas Day, having saved here and there for the treat, we halted in the blazing sunshine to down the last decent meal we should have, seal's liver and bacon and biscuit topped with jam, followed—a surprise I'd contrived myself— by a plum pudding I'd concealed in a spare sock. Next day snow blindness struck Wilson, who twisted in agony and had to be led forward blindfolded, and the day after that we crossed eighty-two. Our bolt was all but shot, however, struggle a few more miles south for a day or two further though we did, and on the last day of the year, dwarfed by the great range of mountains that loomed ahead, more than four hundred miles yet from the Pole, we staggered to the lip of an enormous chasm we knew we could not cross. I photographed Scott there, a tiny figure leaning longingly into the boundless desolation; and then, without a word—

By God, I still hate to admit it. . . .

Then we turned . . . turned in our tracks; we turned back.

Now the true nightmare began. Near what seemed the limit of our endurance we faced a return march of five hundred miles under conditions even viler than those we'd just survived. Temperatures plunged. Clarence died and had to be butchered and fed to his fellows, then Spud, after a terrible day of whining and wheezing on the sledge; while the rest of the dogs, trailing the sledges we three now pulled entirely ("a very striking example," Scott murmured, "of the cart before the horse"), remained worthless dead weight we still lacked the stomach to abandon. Navigation was agony. An almost ceaseless round of blowing snow obliterated the tracks out we were trying to follow, and during the brief times it cleared, great banks of churning fog replaced them. Now and then we gained a few hours' precious respite from hauling when the wind steadied enough to let us hoist sail to the sledge, but more often than not we had it all to do ourselves. Our arms and legs cramped in the night, and the friction of the sledge straps raised ugly round sores on our shoulders.

Worse still was the rapid decline in our health. By now Scott's scurvy had swollen his ankles and loosened his teeth, and Wilson could no more hide his limp or his squint than I could my cough; but I—Ernest Shackleton: sailor, strong man, youngest, tallest, sturdiest, toughest—I was sicker by far. I cursed at my weakness and chewed at my lip, I swore by Ulysses and vowed to go on, anapest, anapest, diddle-um, doo; but I coughed all day, coughed all night, stumbled, fell, spat and spewed blood on the snow, and to level my breath pumped my chest like a bellows, now in, now out, now in. . . . And my mind's eye saw nothing but *meat.*

To strive, to seek, to find . . .

. . . *and not to yield.*

I drove myself on chanting tag ends of verse: Tennyson, Browning, King Henry at Agincourt, anapests, dactyls and iambs and worse, muscle and sinew and big boastful slogans—

But in fact we were *starving,* on rations we'd calculated should cover the work and which we'd conserved conscientiously, dividing the pemmican and cocoa and biscuit with meticulous care, ounce by ounce, meal by meal; and as the cold deepened and the surface coarsened we grew weaker daily. Breaking camp in the morning took longer and longer; our mileages fell; and at last the remaining dogs, poor whimpering skeletons, had to be led off and killed. Scott and I wept together, tears freezing our eyelashes, as the shots from Wilson's pistol rang out one by one across that hideous silence.

It was a near thing, a tight thing, a thing a day or two's difference could have brought out against us, for as it was we only got in by a hairsbreadth. By the end of January I was done, I was *done,* too feeble any longer to keep up my share; and though I argued and begged I had finally to give in to Scott's order I ride on the sledge. That morning I'd overheard Wilson tell him my scurvy was so bad I might die that very afternoon, whereupon I staggered outside and swore I'd outlive them both; but I couldn't go on and I knew it and hated it, and that day and the next I had to let *them,* sad bloody sick sods though they were themselves, push *me.* Scott saved my life, for a fact, but no number of muscular meters could hide the humiliation he made me face to do it; and I cannot forgive him for that.

But he wasn't done yet, no, not Scott, for as we crawled back to base to the cheers of our waiting companions, who'd dressed the *Discovery* with bunting to welcome us in, we spied through the colors the masts of our relief ship, the *Morning,* lying by off the ice; and after a few days' blessed sleep and mountains of food he came 'round to tell me—whose pride wasn't stung deep enough already—that though he and the rest would stay on south another year I should have to go home to get well. . . .

Talk about fetching coals to Newcastle or piling Pelion on Ossa!

Oh, I know he meant best by me, did what he believed to be right; but he reckoned his Irishman wrong.

For I also know this: it wasn't my gifts or my knowledge or my curiosity about the unknown that made me an explorer; it was Scott. I'd gone out an adventurous youngster with a knack for sail and an eye for the main chance, but I came away blooded and seasoned and angry and determined to go back. . . . So if he'd got what he wanted—to be rid of my noxious plebeian pres-

ence 'mongst the quality—well, so for that matter had
I, if at a cost I could wish weren't so high; and by the
time I reached England I knew my true destiny—

To return, to the Pole, my own man with my own
men, and the sooner the better.

I'd truckled my last to the toffs, and I hit London
fighting, well again, healed again, lusty and ready—
and discovered at once it was going to be harder to swing
than I'd thought. The Navy had the money and Scott
had the glory, and few cared to hear the vainglorious
ambitions of a poor Irish sailor who'd been invalided
home. But I stuck with it, made the rounds, and presently found I had powers I'd not known I possessed
(though a bit of reflection on my nights spinning yarns
with the crew would've brought it to mind). I could
gab, I could lecture, I could keep an audience of a hundred or a thousand on the edge of their chairs with my
tales of adventure aboardship, in the pack, on the ice.
They listened, they liked it, liked me, but best of all
they *paid;* and soon, my pockets jingling with cash, I
took to the stage in dead earnest (no pun) and with an
ease that surprised me, going here, there, and everywhere with my slides and my blarney, not only London
and Southport but Aberdeen and Dundee, ladling out
the melodrama and the charm smooth as cream over
strawberries. I met people too, rich men, men with
power and pull, the first of their sort I'd known, and I
nurtured their friendliness and interest and tucked them
away against the day I could use them. Then I wrote a

bit as well and found I had a way with a page also, giving them a shot of Browning here and a touch of old Marryat there, keeping the narrative moving and myself, modest me, in the background. It worked and it helped, not just Shackleton but the war chest he was building.

Still, it was shillings and pence against the real funds I needed, not only to go back but to get by till I did, for I was out of a true job, the kind that pays the grocer, and to add to my problems, what I couldn't just do on my fees, somewhere along I'd decided to get married. Her name was Emily Dorman. We'd met years before and become quite attached, all through my sailing days and then while I was south, and though she was older than me by a bit, she was pretty as peaches and as smart as Bill Wilson; and well off too, praise Pat. But the money was her father's, and anyway I had no desire to be kept; and when Sir Arthur Pearson offered me a subeditorship on his *Royal Magazine* I determined straightaway to accept.

I wanted it all—fame, fortune, position, to be leader, lover, poet, hero—and I wanted it quickly, at once; so for a year or two there I went about like a madman, casting out one line after another to see what would bite, articles, verses, editing, lecturing, a spell as secretary to the Royal Scottish Geographical Society, even a brief turn standing for Parliament (which I lost, but no matter: if I didn't get the votes I at least had the fun, and Shane Leslie told me afterward I was the only speaker in England who could light up an audience as brightly as his plump cousin Winston).... Yes, and then Emily had a baby, we settled into a house and I made friends by the yard.

But the vision persisted, dream or nightmare, Terra Australis, the white and the waste of it, the cold and the struggle, and sometimes after an evening of company and talk, brandy and blather and tall tales and poetry, old pals in from sailing days, old comrades from the *Discovery,* I'd lie awake until dawn, eyes probing the darkness, seeing it plain again, feeling the bite.... Mortification: I'd failed there, fallen short, broken down in the test; and, say what I would for the good life I'd come to—and it was, oh, it was—I couldn't shake free of the itch to go back.

For the matter remained: the Pole still stood virgin, and sooner or later I must try it . . .

. . . or die.

Call me vain, call me proud, call me romantic, quixotic; I *had* to go, *had* to make good, for Emily and England, for myself; and by 1906 I was at it for fair, drawing plans, begging money, searching out ship, stores and crew. I wrote it all out too, proposal and estimate, and sent the result around, hoping to cash in at last on the friendships I'd formed; and though the funds scarcely returned in a torrent, I sensed enough interest to feel confident I could proceed. Beardmore helped, a Clydeside builder I'd got to knew well, and Emily's circle and others, and bit by bit, gifts, pledges and loans began to accumulate. Nor did I mince words as to what I was after: I would go for the Pole, using ponies, dogs, and an auto, and such science as resulted would be but a sideshow. I made it explicit, throwing in the prospect of our stout Union Jack flapping snappily where no flag had flown before, and the businessmen liked that.

But the Navy toffs didn't, and neither did Scott. He was back with the Fleet by then but clearly hankering to go south again himself, and when word reached him that the Mick was on the move he reacted with a roar. So did Markham, and for a time I was as busy arguing and defending as I was planning and panhandling. The nut of their complaint was that McMurdo Sound and the old *Discovery* base belonged by priority to Scott, so that for me to launch my assault there, as I purposed, would be to invade Scott's preserve—and the truth was that to Markham I was still Scott's subordinate, whose venture of independence fell not far short of mutiny. . . . Presumptuous, he thought me, disrespectful, rebellious. No doubt had I been in the Navy he'd've seen I got a taste of the cat.

Life's a struggle, that's what. I no more believed Scott had a "claim" on Antarctica than I believed pigs could fly or penguins do needlepoint, for the unique feature of an unexplored region was and is that it's up for grabs to the fellow sharp enough and plucky enough to strike first, fastest and surest, whoever he is and wherever he comes from; but my success in raising support depended on what good name I had and what good will it engendered, and Markham and Scott had the power to blacken me irreparably if I fought them too bitterly; so in the end I had to play the game and do the sporting thing, sour as it went down, conceding Scott's priority and agreeing to base my own venture elsewhere. It was a devil's bargain, though, a bargain I hated and felt myself forced to, and I've lived to regret it.

Moreover it was a compromise sooner made than kept, as I knew straightaway, but in the rush of completing my preparations I put it out of my mind and focussed my energies on the details instead; and it all came together too, money, men, a ship and supplies, almost suddenly once I gave way to the toffs—the *Nimrod,* a sturdy old sealer I'd run down off Newfoundland, Frank Wild from the *Discovery,* Adams and Marshall and Joyce, Professor David and Douglas Mawson out of Australia, Marston and Dunlop and Day and others, all able and energetic, sledges from Norway, ponies from Tientsin, dogs from New Zealand, an Arrol-Johnston motor car donated by Beardmore, the best of instruments, bought, borrowed and given, and tons of good food of all sorts and varieties. . . . Remembering with a pang those nightmare weeks on the Barrier with Scott and Wilson, I paid special attention to the food.

Supplies aren't everything, though. Some say I'm haphazard, and perhaps the final details of my arrangements were, but in one respect at least I touch my forelock to no commander—I gave my boys *spirit,* gave them the bustle and energy and optimism I felt myself;

and, praise Pat, you could see it at work as we made off
at last, for they had the *Nimrod* twinkling when the
King and Queen came aboard at Cowes to wish us God-
speed, and their eyes gleamed and their bodies snapped
as they turned to the tasks we faced as we moved into
open water and set our sights south. They grinned and
whistled and sang in the shrouds, and at night our lamps
burned late as we talked and smoked and envisioned our
triumph. No prim Navy pecking order for us—we were
a happy ship, a ship bound for glory, and they all called
me Boss.

The good will continued too. New Zealand, where
we spent the end of the year taking on the dogs and
ponies, gave us money and men and quantities of addi-
tional food, cheese and dried milk and butter and a flock
of live sheep, and the hospitality we found amongst its
people would have turned the heads of Drake's rascals.
Professor David joined us in Lyttelton, we broke the
ponies to the sledges, we posted our farewell letters
home; and then, the first day of 1908, to the cheers of
what seemed all New Zealand, we cast off our lines and
headed southward for sure. It was a tender time. "Hearts
of oak are our ships," sang the bluejackets, and finally,
as we dropped the horizon, "Auld Lang Syne" . . .

Terra Australis, Terra Incognita—I was returning
at last, and this time to *win*.

Well, so high was my reach. My grasp, bless Bob, was
something else and something less, and were my nature
as melancholy as Scott's I'd've seen an omen of ill for-

tune in the severity of the weather we encountered almost at once. For weeks we pitched and rolled in seas
wilder than I'd known the world held, manning the
pumps as the winds rose to hurricane force; and we'd
scarcely survived that when, far sooner that I'd foreseen, we sighted icebergs ahead and a day or two afterward entered the pack. That augured a harsh and difficult winter to come, I know now, for early ice forming
well out to sea can mean nothing other than deep cold
and relentless wind on the continent itself; but at the
time my excitement on seeing the bright white breast
of Antarctica again was still so great it forced all thought
of trouble, let alone of failure, from my mind. The
clarity of air! The sharpness of color! The majesty and
the mystery of the Barrier!

Perhaps I lost my judgment then; or perhaps I'd reckoned wrong. My plan—forced on me by the mad, bad
bargain I'd struck with Markham and Scott—was to sail
eastward along the Barrier edge until somewhere off
King Edward VII Land I found a cove or bight or inlet
suitable for anchorage with sufficient rock beside and
beneath to permit establishment of a safe, stable base.
. . . But floating ice was everywhere, breaking off in
huge bergs that threatened to crush us from every side
and in whatever course we tried to take, while the Barrier itself, rising in hummocks and undulations and
peaks of ice and snow in every direction, proved time
and again—beat against it however I sought—beyond
my ability to penetrate. I could find no rock, no land, no

inlet in which to hide and bide and anchor, nor—no matter what the pact—could I expose the lives of forty trusting men to the danger of a base built on ice that might at any instant break away and plunge them into the sea; so that at last, exhausted, heartsore, I had to give it up and turn away, turn back, to safety, to security—

To McMurdo Sound . . .

. . . What else could I do?

We made it there by the very nick too, through ice now hardening rapidly, and at Cape Royds, twenty miles north of the old *Discovery* base at Hut Point, I satisfied myself that enough rock lay underfoot to let us build a stable station . . . yes; but for me it was only dust and ashes, the gilt had gone off the gingerbread, for— though I'd used my wits and spared my boys—I'd done what I'd said I wouldn't, I'd gone back on my word, and the knowledge of that betrayal, unavoidable as I kept telling myself it was, ate my guts out. (What would Scott have done?) We landed ourselves and our kit and dug into the work, and I held up my head as I showed them the way . . . yes; but it was all bluster, all show, and I knew it. I ached. Something had broken, inside, where the spirit lives. (*What would Wilson have done?*)

There was my standard, then, and I judged myself by it. Yet I had to go on as well, for the rest if no longer altogether for myself, and by whistling and singing and slapping their backs I recovered at least some of the cheer I knew how to bestow; and as we went along into winter I began to feel the pitch and sway of the thing again too, all swagger aside . . . for off there to the south, across the Barrier and beyond the purple mountains, lay what we'd come for, the patch unseen, the place, the point, the Pole. I set myself for it and put all else from my mind.

Well, but reach and grasp, *et cetera.* . . . My mind refused to let it—"all else"—go; and though throughout the working day I went ahead briskly, doing my share and more, hauling, building, sledging, planning, taking the lead and setting the pace, as soon as I fell idle the awful accusation of disloyalty returned, nagging my leisure and wrecking my sleep. I tightened the task, therefore, driving myself and the rest to what sometimes seemed the very brink of exhaustion; with the result, though I say so who shouldn't, that we accomplished more and held our health better than any expedition before us. The scientists accumulated all manner of data (beyond my ken, but never mind); one of our parties scaled and surveyed old smoking Erebus; Professor David and Mawson readied preparations for seeking the South Magnetic Pole; and in the hut we ate ourselves hearty from the fare I'd seen to providing. Challenge invigorates men; their strength rises to meet it— I'd learned that from Scott; and, private blessing, it holds back the night and the solitude . . .

. . . and the guilt.

Meanwhile that other night, the long Antarctic winter's night, began to shorten and wane, and with the slow return of the feeble springtime dawn I settled to the last of my own necessities; for our chance of making the Pole rested, I knew, as much on the earliness of our start as on the thoroughness of our preparations. The surface would hold only so long as the light lasted. The sledging season would be brief. I determined to have as much of it as Providence conferred.

Was I ripe, though? Was I ready? Was my heart really in it? No man who like Scott or me goes out to search the dark uncharted corners of the earth can blink the chance of doom—and I faced that, faced death, faced the fact I might fail to win through. What I stumbled at was the other thing, the fear that I'd failed to keep faith; and, strive though I did to soothe my bad conscience, it deviled my thoughts and gnawed at my confidence and sent me off south halfway crippled.

But I offer no alibi. My self-doubt was private. I owed my men the optimism I'd asked of them; and as we moved away in the brilliant sunshine of a late October morning I cheered them on who could no longer cheer himself. Wild, Marshall and Adams were my companions, the best of an excellent lot, and together we pushed the ponies to a sledging speed that boded well for the struggle ahead. So did the weather, which for four weeks gave us bright windless days and a hard surface crust that eased and hastened our path through and past the maze of crevasses that crisscrossed the Barrier. We marched and hauled as one. Our mileages doubled and trebled the distances of 1902 and '03, and by the end of November we had passed Scott's Furthest South, a month ahead to boot.

Call that much luck. There too it ended; or perhaps there my retribution began. Chinaman, the oldest of the ponies, chafed his fetlocks and had to be shot. The surface softened, making it agony to lift our tired feet from the snow. Then Grisi, snow blind and weakening, stumbled and fell and had to be killed. Our legs felt the Barrier rise. Most daunting of all, however, was the steep wall of mountain ahead; I could see no way round it.

Well, at least my nerve was intact. I struck out instead for a polar route *through,* staking our fate on the chance of a gateway neither I nor anyone had seen or could be certain was there; and, praise Pat, I found it, beyond the red granite ridge on which I'd set my bearings, an immense glacier trending south between the ranges and pointing like an arrow, where perspective brought its sides together sixty miles ahead, dead on at the Pole. Blue ice it was, silted up with snow, cruel and treacherous to sledge on, yes, but sloping upward so evenly I was sure it must lead us at last past the mountains to the plateau on which, I now knew, the Pole itself stood. We roped our way onto it and there turned off south.

. . . Perilous going, but going it was; and we took heart from that. Then occurred what proved the gravest of our disasters. We'd had to kill Quan at the end of the Barrier, but Socks, the last of the ponies, continued strong and, though the crust could not always hold him and he often sank to his belly in the snow, his power with the sledges helped us hold our precious speed. But one early December midday, making for the better surface at the center of the glacier, he suddenly vanished, *whoosh,* and Wild and the sledge after him. We other three were at the spot in an instant and managed quickly to haul Wild and the sledge to safety from the crevasse into which they'd been plunged, but Socks was gone, had disappeared in the black depth below, snapped from his traces without warning or sound.

No doubt that was the point at which I should've recognized the eventual futility of our mission, and perhaps then the realist underneath knew we should never succeed in planting the Queen's flag at the bottom of the world; for besides all else, besides strength and purpose and pluck and luck, we needed the remaining horsemeat Socks would've provided when his sledging power ceased—our packed rations were calculated on that contingency. . . . But failure was something I still couldn't face, not yet, not then, not when I'd just pioneered a landfall that must lead to the very triumph I'd come south to claim—

So I pushed myself on and pulled the others with me. We had to move by relay now, marching six miles for every two we actually advanced, while the hard, slick surface of the glacier thwarted every effort we made to improve our declining daily average. All of us bore bruises everywhere, and the sledges were nicked and

battered and their runners bent from the spills we took;
but by some precious mercy no one broke a limb or
suffered a flesh wound and the sledges held together.
By another the weather held too, colder steadily and at
night, with our body fat vanishing, almost too painful to
endure, but clear and windless by day and with nothing
yet falling. So we moved, moved ahead, and our hopes
rose. . . .

False hopes, vain hopes; for speed was essential if we
were to last out our food, and with Socks gone our mileages fell drastically, ten miles a day, eight, six, then
five and three; and our rations fell with them. So I cut
our daily intake, saving two biscuits a day and a portion
of pemmican and sugar against the longer march we
now faced in and back, and we struggled on that way
through December, climbing with the glacier. By then
our altitude stood at more than eight thousand feet; we
passed eighty-five degrees; and still the glacier rose. I
had seriously underestimated its height.

Christmas Day found us seemingly nearing its summit, though, with the wind rising and the temperature
falling, and at noon we broke our morning's march and
feasted, so to say, on the bits and bites we'd hoarded for
the occasion, extra cheese and cocoa and a special hoosh
of pony meat and biscuit, with a drop of brandy and a
spoonful of crème de menthe apiece to top it off; and
afterward I took their picture against the background of
the peaks, Wild, Adams and Marshall in line, teeth
white as they grinned through their ferocious frozen

beards, sledge flags flapping brightly behind. It was a high time, a happy time; our hearts, like Henry's men's, were in the trim; and that night, convinced by Christmas we still might make the Pole, we agreed to cut our rations further.

Cruel illusion. . . . The surface softened to a finely powdered snow that dogged and clogged each step we took, and though we'd thought ourselves almost to level ground, the New Year came and went and we'd hauled the sledges more than eleven thousand feet above sea level before we came out at last upon the plateau. Our satisfaction in that attainment was scant, however, as it was in knowing that having passed eighty-seven degrees we'd beaten Nansen's Furthest North; for our exhaustion was revealing itself in undeniable debility and slowness on the march and our rations were down to the bone. Then, as if to mock our puny ways, a blizzard struck and held us to the tents.

It passed, of course, but by the time it did our situation was grave. The headache I'd had for weeks was now constant; the others were giddy and short of breath; and Marshall's examination found us all at body temperatures so far below normal he insisted we return to regular rations. Outside we faced a fierce head wind and drifting snow and the thermometer showed fifty degrees of frost. We could go on a day by forced march, and we did; and another, and we did; and another. . . .

But then?

But then I had to face the final harsh but telling

truth. With luck and a last good burst of strength our rations would take us to the Pole; but they would never make that extra distance back. We could seize the spot and claim the triumph . . . yes—

But had to die to do so.

No leader yet, no Drake or Raleigh, no, nor Scott, could boast such men as I had with me then. I sought their weary faces, there, in the tent, and they gave it all back to me, the long years of yearning, the struggle and the striving; and by their silent smiles they let me make the judgment for them. They would do as I wished, as I said; I was Boss.

. . . Well, a part of me was willing, would have died to do the thing regardless, and I heard it speak, that Irish devil, brogue, brag and all, heard my pride claim its prize. . . . But then, though vain and selfish, I was only I, after all, and there was and is more to the world than myself; there were others. I could not let them die to serve my glory.

Besides, besides . . . there'd be tomorrow.

So that last day down we ran out together, four tattered madmen in the snow, sledges left behind as we sprinted southward till our lungs broke, then halting at last because we could run, walk or stagger no further; and there, the wind singing past us, we planted Her Majesty's flag where no flag had ever flown, past any man's reach, past even Scott's. The sun came in to give us eighty-eight degrees and twenty-three minutes South. We were fewer than a hundred miles from the Pole. . . .

And there we turned back.

We would live, and we did; and we do; and someday, praise Pat, I'll return, go again, not for the Pole itself, perhaps, for by then someone else will have done the thing we four came so close to doing, but to *cross* Antarctica, Terra Australis, sea to sea, *through* the Pole—now there's a dream to plan on!

And if, bless Bob, I fail?

Well . . .

. . . what's a heaven for?

# AMUNDSEN

1911

LEAVE NOTHING TO CHANCE. It could serve as my epitaph. I stand now at the point toward the attainment of which I have bent every effort of my life. As a place in itself it is nothing or less, flat, bleak, sere, so hazy we must use an artificial horizon for our sextants, to the eye indistinguishable from countless others here and elsewhere on this great but mostly empty globe we all inhabit. Yet, in truth, the world holds no other like it, none, and to fix it precisely and incontestably my companions and I have sighted and shot and triangulated it until no man alive or yet to live can question the authenticity of our bearings. I turn this way, that, and the index reading never changes by so much as a hairsbreadth of a degree. . . . We have succeeded. We are there. We have reached the single point in all the universe where there is no direction but north.

My colleagues express some small exhilaration at the fact, by laconic winks and nods and elbow nudges revealing their excited satisfaction, and to do them the honor they deserve—for the accomplishment is as thoroughly theirs as mine—I join their little moment, shaking their hands and offering each the threadbare commonplaces of congratulation by which, like other humans, we contrive to reduce the magnitude of great events to the triviality of a football match. Yet my gestures are gestures only, for I feel myself no sporting triumph in our arrival. We are here because we arranged it so: because we planned it, organized it and saw it to its execution through a thousand tedious details, and toward the consummation of so completely conceived a program, I find it impossible to direct so paltry an emotion as joy. My own satisfaction, if not theirs, lies deeper: in the knowledge that by the identification and elimination of every imaginable contingency, I have foreseen and thus forestalled what other men regard as the unforeseeable risks of chance.

But chance is the romantic fantasia of schoolboys playing at exploration. They pursue it like knights in quest of the Grail, with the significant qualification that for them the quest and its dangers are the reality, not the Grail. These Englishmen who've sought and seek the Poles are such, Captain Scott, his rival Shackleton,

Franklin before them, and though I can no more resist
their chivalrous charm and good spirit than the rest of
the world, I privately find them, as least as explorers, no
better than jolly sportsmen. Like their swashbuckling
forebears Raleigh and Drake, they love to cut a pretty
figure, love to win the hearts and bring sentimental tears
to the eyes of their insular countrymen (and women),
who see them, no doubt, as heroes of empire, braving
the risks of the unknown to bear England's green peace
to the furthermost reaches of the world's vast wilderness.
They court risks with smiles that bring their handsome
faces to a glow, and they make lovely legends. Myself,
I take no risks, I win no hearts, I have no women and I
make no legends. I am Amundsen, I am Norse: my forebear is Leif Ericson, not Raleigh, and though I daresay
he was as homely as I, he was first to make Vinland, as I
am first to make this Pole.

It is a coup to have got here, the coup I intended,
and there can be no convincing argument otherwise; yet
I scarcely need flatter myself or my prestige that no argument will ensue. To the English the only satisfactory
world is an English world, a world explored by English
sailors, settled by English outcasts and administered by
English civil servants; they will neither sleep nor rest
until they have turned every map red and hoisted their
hearty Union Jack above every capital on it. It is their
special conceit to have it so, the game they play when
they have laid aside their cricket bats; they prefer to be
first, indeed they take it as their due, and the fact that in

coming here I have bested one of their own will not go down well. He is out there somewhere now, Captain Scott, struggling with his worthless sledges and foolish ponies against the snow and the wind and the cold, and perhaps if he's lucky—for without dogs he will have to be lucky—one day soon he'll step into the horizon and find we've forestalled him; then the furor will follow. Above all men I feel for his disappointment—more to the point, I pray for his survival—but all that is immaterial. For, say what they will about their love of a contest, the English are poor losers. Never mind that I wintered in the Antarctic before Scott knew it existed, nor that my conquest of the Northwest Passage established my cachet as an explorer; never mind that I gave him full notice of my plans, nor that at the Bay of Whales I offered his men up to half of my dogs. I made it here first, beat Scott, beat them all, and for that they will bestow upon me their worst epithet. They will call me unsporting.

Be that as it may, I have stuck to my plan, tendering both its dangers and uncertainties such respect as my long experience demonstrates they deserve. Exploration may be adventure to some but it is life itself to me, the calling to which I have devoted the thought, the energy, the discipline and the sacrifice of nearly a quarter of a century; and now that they have eventuated in this moment I do not propose to leave the triumph—for, adventure or calling, to reach the South Pole first is a triumph, and mine—open to challenge. Detached though it seems, science is jealous, holding its practitioners and their tiniest claims to the strictest account; however profound my personal satisfaction at our location, I scarcely dare expose my findings unverified. I mean no immodesty when I say that thoroughness is the essence of my nature.

For that reason, as well as because I want no repetition of the sordid controversy that soiled the achievements of Burton and Speke, I have directed a painstaking survey of the entire Polar area. Bjaaland, Wisting, Hassel, Hanssen and I have struck forth and followed a series of radii for as much as ten miles from where our sextants first showed the Pole to be, at each point taking new sightings, recording our measurements, finally setting out flags, or at any rate planting skis bearing the only flags we could fashion, long strips of black burlap that we'd ripped, methodically, into the semblance of pennants. By such means we have formed a perimeter around the Pole, which by triangulation must lie, where I stand, at the convergence of our lines; and here we have erected a tent, small but sturdy and supported by a single bamboo, in which to leave a record of our presence: a few instruments, a deposition of our attainment, a letter to King Haakon and a covering note to Scott, asking him to deliver it should I fail—and he manage—to return. This is a conceit, of course. I do not intend to fail.

Wisting smiles, the best of good companions and also the ablest, and we raise our country's flag above our little tent, claiming this land, these parts, for Norway; another conceit, perhaps, for no nation could pretend seriously to own or control so desolate a place as this. Nor is territorial acquisition a Norwegian custom; we leave that to the English, who covet the map. Still, to make such a claim is traditional, no doubt in this case harmlessly so, and now that the thing is done I find I take pleasure in the spectacle of the Norse standard aflutter where no flag has flown before. It is reminiscent of the Union Jack, our neat blue cross piped white against a scarlet field, but a measure less flamboyant, a measure more modest, I fancy; a third conceit, to which I permit myself a moment's indulgence. Then we step back a pace and offer it a brief salute.

The wind has risen, out of what I was about to think of as the east, forgetting—so curious is the realization—that here there is no east, no west, no longer any south; and we turn to keep its cutting edges from our eyes, our faces, which despite our care are badly burned. Above us the sun is a milky lozenge, available to our sextants but useless as a source of heat, and at the sight of it I shiver, not from the cold—for I have long since taught my body to accept that—but from the thought that to win this goal we have put ourselves beyond the reach of man's accustomed comforts. A shadow falls. . . . The world remains, but by our indifference to its dangers we have revealed as well its indifference to us. Life is more precarious than most men know.

None, I think, has known it better or longer than I, who was called to exploration as a boy, but even I have had to learn it for myself. As children we were secure, my older brothers and I, snug, smug in our endowments, well cared for, well protected, set smoothly on the way to the safe attainments of our station and class. Our home and hearth were happy, and in the ordinary course of things our lives would take such shape as custom warranted: the pulpit, business, law. I was myself to study medicine, and indeed—for one did as one was told—I took my turn in the dissecting room and laboratory, memorizing bones and nerves and tissues with the rest. But secretly my mind was elsewhere. At fifteen, seemingly by chance, I came upon Sir John Franklin's account of his attempt, half a century before, to find the Northwest Passage; and from that moment on I had no other thought. My imagination teemed with pictures far removed from the steady rounds of the practitioner: I saw myself, like Franklin, struggling alone against the awesome silent stretches of the Arctic, yet with the difference, characteristic of me, that though I found the dangers thrilling I sought no martyrdom like his. To me they were a challenge to be overcome by discipline, by training my mind and toughening my body; and while by day I dutifully did my stint as novice healer, by night I made my plans. For even at fifteen my ambition was clear: I would find the Northwest Passage, find the North Pole, find whatever else there was to find around the unknown Arctic reaches of the world. I would succeed where Franklin, and all the innumerable others, had failed.

Bold thoughts, presumptuous thoughts . . . and had

my father lived, with his wholly worldly bent and his
grumpy disesteem for what he saw as pretentious nonsense, I should have found him a formidable opponent to
their realization. But he died while I was still a student,
and my mother, who in her doting affection believed me
diligent, was easy to deceive. In fact I was as industrious
as she imagined, deep in books long after she herself
was sleeping, except that the books I studied so intently
were the annals of polar exploration rather than the
texts on *materia medica* she supposed. I had always mastered information quickly, could record and organize it
almost as rapidly as my eyes ran the page, so that an
hour or so an evening was usually time enough to keep
up my assignments; and after that I regarded myself as
free to read and ponder what I liked. Thus before I was
twenty I had assimilated the better part of what had
then been written on the Arctic, knew the journeys and
findings of the Cabots, Chancellor, Burrough, Barents,
Carlsen, Davis, Scoresby, Franklin, Nordenskjold, De
Long and Greely more intimately than the precepts of
Hippocrates and Harvey, and had begun, as well, to
form my own conclusions of their worth. But it was a
double life I led, pretending to prepare for one profes-
sion when in reality I was readying myself for another,
and as I neared the moment when I must commit my
plans irrevocably, I grew increasingly restive, distracted
and irritable. Ordinarily my disposition is even, but
hypocrisy sat poorly on my conscience. I preferred truth
plain, not disguised. I would have made a dismal doctor.

As events determined, however, I did not have to make that particular discovery at some poor patient's expense. Abruptly, without warning, my mother died too; and though I grieved for her then and ever afterward, I could not suppress my relief at being able, at last, to abandon deception. Within weeks I had quit the university forever and was deep, but without dissemblance, in preparation for the work to which I had already committed my imagination and allegiance.

By that time my master was Nansen, Fridtjof Nansen, to whose extraordinary work and inspiring example every Arctic explorer is fundamentally indebted, for my reading had convinced me that his care for detail and his ability to reason from it must hold the solution to crucial Polar problems; but he had just left Norway aboard the *Fram* on what was to prove the most significant expedition of his career, and for that matter mine. So in his absence I turned elsewhere: first to a rigid program of physical conditioning, then—once I had achieved a level of strength and stamina that I was satisfied would do— to the attainment of a maritime captain's license. Neither proved beyond me. Thanks to a lucky heredity, I suppose, I had always been healthy and sturdy, and a diligent regimen of hiking, camping, football and, above all, skiing quickly brought me to a degree of muscular fitness that I have been able to maintain ever since; its corollary was that by exposing myself to the cold in all weathers, especially by always sleeping out of doors, I habituated my body—and, of equal importance, my mind—to the extreme low temperatures I would experience in the Arctic. So much was obvious. Where I took an original step of my own was to learn to sail.

Let the English roll dice with destiny. Ignorance and disorder, I say, will yield only to reason. . . .

We Norse have been seafarers since the dawn of time, of course, and in common with most of my countrymen I grew up with and near and on the water; but now I needed more than the mere sporting skills required to handle small craft. Again and again, in my study of exploration, I had been struck by what I came slowly to recognize was a fatal weakness in the organization of Polar parties: the division of command between the explorer, himself, and the captain of his ship. Though on the open sea this may have been of no consequence, once the expedition entered uncharted Arctic waters, two factions invariably emerged, two contrary and eventually conflicting sets of loyalties, and in the succeeding vacuum of authority the explorer and his staff were left, inevitably, at the mercy of the captain and his crew, who—fearing the hazards of the ice, which they assessed only too accurately, and lacking any inner commitment to the quest of the unknown—more often than not turned aside or turned back. This was understandable but to me intolerable, and I determined to avoid it. If I were to explore the Arctic successfully I must have sole authority. I must be not only explorer but navigator. I must be not only navigator but captain. I must and I would—

*—Leave nothing to chance.*

There, then, again; if not my epitaph, at least my credo. . . . Whereupon Wisting smiles, as if reading my mind, for he knows, knows me, knows I am not ready, not yet, to write my epitaph.

Well, so I did what I had to do, took papers, put myself before the mast, learned the seaman's hard trade the hard way but only way, and presently, by such means, I was ready: could read a chart and shoot the sun and plot and keep a course with the saltiest; and was thus able, at twenty-five, to ship as first mate with the Belgian expedition to survey and study the South Magnetic Pole —an irony, surely, the first but by no means the last, for though it has been my lifelong aim to be first at the North Pole, it has been my lifelong lot to come repeatedly to the South.

My lot, my luck, my destiny, my fate. . . . But I reject fate, I disbelieve in it as I disbelieve in chance and its fickle dispensations, for in fact my deliberate preparations had equipped me for either, for North Pole and South Pole alike. And so I was ready. Locked in the ice, half-mad with scurvy, the expedition foundered, command falling to me. From my reading I had concluded that fresh meat must hold the cure, and with the American physician Cook, today so discredited, I dug from the snow a quantity of seal carcasses, which we then cut into steaks to feed our prostrate shipmates; they recovered. Thus too with the ice, from which, again with Cook, I planned and effected our deliverance, by cutting and finally blasting a channel to the warmer melting waters of the open sea. Thus also with our navigation of the Straits of Magellan, where by recognizing Church Island, of which I had read as a boy, I, alone, was able to find a way through. . . .

Gross immodesty, no doubt, to remember such feats, let alone to dwell upon them; yet at this moment of triumph I remind myself, as I must, how little I owe the Pole and its conquest to luck, to destiny, to fate—or to chance. For they will call me lucky, the English will, as ages ago they did my forebear. . . .

Leif the Lucky, *Amundsen the Lucky*—their way of explaining defeat, I suppose.

The flag of Norway snaps suddenly, cracking the silence like a pistol shot, and at the sound the dogs stir restlessly from their exhausted daydreams, apprehensive of a signal they have learned long since must mean another death amongst their dwindling number. Then, more anxious yet, they begin to whimper, to whine, at last to bay. I step across, past Bjaaland, and stoop to pat Lasse, my favorite of them all. His enormous molten eyes are affectionate but resigned, for he feels what I feel, thus knows what I know, that he has worn himself weary beyond recovery or further usefulness and therefore, tomorrow, must die. I chuck his chin, murmuring the indefinable words through which by now we have said so much between us, and finally he shudders and sighs and lowers his head, slumberous again. He has performed nobly, bravely, more generously than even I could have foreseen, who raised him from a pup, and in his honor, when the time comes, I shall do the thing myself, cleanly and painlessly, afterward dividing his princely carcass into fifteen equal portions: it will be his final good service, as I believe he knows, to provide a hearty meal for his remaining companions. But I am a sentimental man too, however practical, and I shall hope always to remember him with the esteem he deserves.

Still, I separate sentiment from necessity, and poor Scott would do well to do likewise. Nansen taught me that, and much else, on my return from Antarctica. By then he was back in Norway himself, safe, sound and triumphantly vindicated in his belief, at which established science had scoffed, that a persistent ocean current flows from the Arctic coastland of Siberia across the top of the world, past the North Pole and thence southward around Greenland. The chain of reasoning by which he had arrived at that conviction and the practical, irrefutable experiment by which he had demonstrated its validity held the profoundest consequences for Polar studies and for me, for Nansen had argued that the otherwise inexplicable presence of Siberian timber in Greenland, where no trees grow, must in fact mean they had drifted there on a current previously unrecognized and uncharted; then by locking the *Fram* in the icepack off Cape Chelyushkin and letting it drift where it would, he had come out, in the end, at Spitzbergen, as he foresaw. The meticulous logic of that approach, so methodical, so thorough, contrasted strikingly, to my taste, with the slapdash adventurism of the English; of equal significance to me was Nansen's successful use of dog teams and lightweight sledges for quick travel across the ice itself, for I saw in it, what the English would not, a way to attack the Pole, when my time came, free of the Arctic explorer's immemorial dependence on a self-defeatingly burdensome cargo of foodstuffs. Ponies, so favored by the English, require transported fodder; but dogs, thriving on dried fish, seal meat, whale meat, even dog meat, can live off the land. I have Nansen to thank for that knowledge, a Norseman, a Viking, as well as for his extraordinary example of diligence, steadiness and realism. It is what has put me here today—and left Scott who knows where out there in the snow.

Thenceforward my course was clear, not merely the goal I sought but the program by which I proposed to accomplish it, awaiting for its consummation only the accumulation of such means as I would need to purchase a ship and supplies and employ a crew; and here too, so to say, Nansen stood wise Virgil to my untutored Dante; providing me, besides the knowledge and encouragement he gave so liberally, the argument I should require to convince the moneymen of what great good sense it would be to invest in my endeavors. Science was in the air, he observed, and with it an almost mystical confidence in its powers; to gain financial support I must therefore persuade my sponsors of the scientific benefits certain to follow successful exploration of the Pole.

Zoologist and oceanographer, Nansen was himself so persuaded and intended no duplicity in urging me to similar faith; while I, though I had and have no more genuine scientific curiosity than a cockroach, only too readily agreed . . . for that matter I would have pleaded the Pole's benefits to ballet or gastronomy had I believed it would raise the money I wanted. Cynicism? Hypocrisy? No doubt. But the common coin of exploration; and at least, unlike Scott, who has ended by believing his own scientific propaganda, I never deluded myself.

. . . The wind shifts, casting tiny snowflakes, sharp as sand, against our checks. No; I tell myself no lies; I am here, ninety degrees south, for the single overpowering reason that I wanted to be here first, where no man had been before. Scott's motive was the same, and still is, if he lives. No explorer, let him claim what he will, has another. There is no other.

Nonetheless I know what it is to be poor, to need money, to dream dreams beyond the reach of one's means, know one must do what one must; and because I do, I played the game, spun the sinuous web of mendacious scientism that would justify my ventures, learned all I could of terrestrial magnetism and the various tedious methods of making magnetic observations, first at Hamburg (since the English had refused to let me study at the British Observatory at Kew), afterward at Wilhelmshaven and Potsdam; and presently, head reeling with dipoles and declinations, I deemed myself ready, in the American expression, to pass the hat. For by now, through relentless analysis, I had anticipated the steps I must take to realize my ultimate plan. To staff and supply an expedition elaborate enough to assault the North Pole I must raise an enormous purse; but to do that I must first make my reputation as an explorer; and to do *that* I must accomplish a feat so dramatic I would capture the attention of the world. . . . Formidable obstacles; yet as it happened such a feat, should I choose it, lay close to hand: the Fata Morgana of every sailor since Magellan, the mariners' vision, the jewel, the prize— the Northwest Passage. . . .

Toward its conquest, however, I attached no such romance; nor suffered the smallest scintilla of doubt that conquer it I could. To my mind it was but a vehicle, a series of points on a chart from one to the next of which, by logic and application, I would navigate my way. I thought of it as a problem in seamanship, an exercise in sailing, and its legendary difficulties as no more than questions to answer. Its romantic mystique simply served my private purpose.

Romantic nomad, sage wizard of science . . . what preposterous personae I have had to assume to do what I wanted! As if to conquer the Pole were not end enough in itself! As if curiosity required rationalization! In fact we explorers are the simplest of men, driven by the most elemental of instincts to sniff our shuffling way from one place to the next, but caring little, after all, what we find when we get there. Yet the rest of mankind asks that we have a good reason. . . . As well ask a dog why it grubs out a garbage heap!

Why have I come here? To get here—no more, no less, no other. Yet by the time I return I shall have had to invent and embellish a dozen more elevated motives. Scott, poor fellow, will at least be spared that; he will not be spared much else. . . .

Well, so I sailed the Northwest Passage as I'd said I would, 'and it went as I'd foreseen it would, no picnic perhaps but of no insuperable difficulty either. My plans were thorough and my calculations exact, and in the *Gjoa,* tiny but seaworthy, I had a vessel that, whatever amusement it afforded others, had proved as a fishing boat to possess those qualities of lightness and maneuverability I needed to navigate the shallow waters and narrow channels I anticipated along the southerly route I proposed to follow. This, too, was heresy, this route, for the accumulated wisdom of established exploration dictated higher latitudes and the broader channels to be found there; but I preferred logic and the chart, which told me I would avoid the worst of the icepacks if I held to the main coast. This I did; and whereas my predecessors had turned back, or were lost, I got through.

It was an easy success, truth to tell, for I had relied throughout on reason and systematic preparation, using my experience as a sailor and my solid familiarity with the work of Franklin, Nansen and Nordenskjold to anticipate every problem and confine it to its essentials, and apart from such minor incidents as can lessen the efficiency of any long voyage—a fire in the hold, an occasional malfunction of one instrument or another—I recall it now as almost uneventful; but to the world at

large, sedentary, restless and fed a daily diet of melo-
dramatic sensationalism by the press, it was a naviga-
tional feat comparable only to Magellan's. Nonsense, of
course, but it was for precisely such nonsense, and for
the support it almost certainly guaranteed, that I had
planned; and I reached the west coast of the United
States to find myself—what my purse needed, if not my
vanity—a popular hero.

The welcome I received in San Francisco could easily
have turned my head, for though I had counted on my
navigation of the Northwest Passage to establish my
credit as an explorer, I had hardly anticipated having to
play matinee idol too; but, my mind churning with far
more ambitious projects than the one I had just concluded, I could not afford to nurture the conceit to which
I was being encouraged. For by now, right or wrong, I
had the strong sense that my time was beginning to run
out. Thanks to me and others, exploration had captured
the imagination of the public. Polar programs were being proposed on all sides, by Germany, Sweden, France
and Russia, not to mention Norway and Britain. Scott's
*Discovery* expedition to the Antarctic, though it had
failed to reach the Pole itself, was as great a popular success as mine, and there was talk he might soon lead another. Shackleton's was already under way. Peary was
busily raising American money to attack the North
Pole, as was Cook, my friend from earlier days. But it
was not the prospect of rivalry alone that disturbed me;
I believed myself an abler explorer, better prepared,

more singly committed, than any of my potential competitors. What gnawed at my confidence was the knowledge that, having passed thirty, I could be assured of few remaining years of the enormous physical vitality I knew I would need to reach the Pole the way I wanted to: on my own.

I had no doubt, however, of the particular program I intended to pursue, for my years of study and apprenticeship had gradually sharpened to the finest point my opinion of the means by which the North Pole should be assaulted; and after a tour of lecturing in the United States and Europe, fees from which repaid my creditors and laid the foundation of a new expeditionary purse, I returned to Norway determined to lose no further time in readying its details. Perhaps any plan that succeeds is a good plan, and indeed the English will say I have reached the South Pole by similar ruthlessness; but the sort of approach by which Peary had so often failed, and which he now indicated he would follow again, held no appeal for me. Going for the Pole head-on, by what amounted to a sophisticated form of dead reckoning, seemed to me little better than exploration by brute force; it lacked, as I saw it, the artistry that gives the work of the great explorers its beauty and finality. Let Peary use his battering ram as he would, I had no intention of stooping to barbarism. I would take the Pole with elegance.

My proposal, in fact, was to complete the classic voyage of Nansen, who despite the authority with which he had demonstrated the truth of his theory of the Arctic current had nonetheless failed to reach the Pole. He had gone Farthest North, to be sure, and of the scientific validity of his experiment there could be no doubt; while by his innovative sledging he had prepared the way for all Polar explorers who followed him. These were achievements of the highest order, distinctive and un-challengeable, and I had no thought of trying to share or diminish them. My intention, instead, was to honor the work of the explorer I most revered by taking it to the conclusion to which its brilliant logic and flawless execution inevitably pointed. By this time, absorbed in other scientific interests and no longer bent on taking the Pole personally, Nansen himself encouraged my pro-gram and used his enormous prestige to ease my access to the sponsors I would need. His generosity and large-mindedness were characteristic, as was his enthusiasm for the ambitions of a colleague some years his junior and by many degrees his inferior; and I think now, as I savor this success of which neither of us dreamed, of his unique unselfishness. He is the single explorer I know— and I include myself—too great to fear rivalry.

My life at this point, unlike Nansen's—which was broad, rich and rounded—contained nothing beyond my work. I had no other interests; my older brothers were at best remote acquaintances, and I had failed to develop an appetite for the fleshly pleasures to which most healthy men of my age gave full rein. My concentration was like a knot. Months passed in which I spent my days and nights in an intensity of attention so exclusive I could scarcely have named the date or recognized a change in the weather. Frequently I worked eighteen and twenty hours without interruption for food or conversation. I read and reread everything printed about Polar currents, conditions and experiences, memorized the smallest details of every chart I could unearth, weighed every possible mode of attack in the light of every imaginable contingency; and from this slowly crystallizing mastery of the material I carefully developed a plan, simple in outline but balanced as subtly and as delicately as a clock, by which to proceed. My habits, like my thoughts, were as austere as a monk's, and it may well be that like a monk I removed myself too far from the stabilizing influence of human fraternity. Wisting believed I ran that danger, at any rate; for on the rare occasion when he could persuade me to break our labors with an hour of coffee or beer in an Oslo cafe, he would chide me laughingly for my monomania, urging me to let myself respond more fully to the ordinary life around us, to let the color, warmth and gaiety of the passersby restore me to my neglected membership in mankind; and now and then as a pretty girl passed or smiled or moved her body or let me catch her scent, I felt to my surprise a flooding of that erotic desire—so natural but to me at that point so threatening —against which I believed I had successfully sealed myself. But the lust passed as the moment passed, and I let it pass. My commitment was single, indivisible and absolute. To conquer the Pole was and must be life enough. I could tolerate neither deviation nor distraction. Afterward, if I survived. . . . But I went no further.

A fault in my character, no doubt, this independence of human satisfactions, like one of those geologic fissures that from time to time sunders the crust of the earth. Yet I make no claim to normality. No explorer could. I say of myself only this: I have done what I said I would.

. . . The wind stirs; the dogs stir; and they stir too, my companions, Wisting's eyes looking their question at me, for having accomplished what they came to do, they are anxious, restless, eager to regain the comforts and securities of a world more familiar than this white waste of snow and ice and nothing else. Well, we differ in that. I am at home here, at peace, for out of the disorder of ignorance I have sought and brought the order of knowledge—the scientist's dream, the artist's dream, and I have lived to realize it. . . .

But the winter is coming, for us, for Scott, and soon we must go. . . .

Now time pressed. Shackleton returned from Antarctica radiant with glory. Peary set off north aboard the *Roosevelt,* lavishly financed and almost suffocatingly sponsored by American interests. Cook sailed too, to less pomp. The English announced with their customary bravado that Scott would lead a new expedition south. . . . And in Oslo I skied, swam, read books, drew charts; and I begged: begged dogs, begged crew, begged money.

I had sense, strength, experience and a plan; but little more. I needed a ship. I needed food. I needed equipment.

*But I was ready:* no detail had escaped my anticipation, no prospective crewman had evaded my persuasion, no supplier of dogs or provisions or kit had eluded my search or refused my demand that he stand alert to meet my requirements on briefest notice—so that instead of cursing the misfortune of my poverty, I reminded myself that I did not believe in fortune, good or bad, that my true fortune lay in my inveterate readiness, when the moment came, to seize its possibilities rather than bewail its tardiness. I was, as Wisting complained, like one of those ecclesiastical eremites who spends his life in preparation for the death that may find him at any instant, with the important exception that I was preparing not for death but for the achievement of my life. . . . A kind of fanaticism too, I suppose, but my kind, my way.

And the moment came. Unconsciously, perhaps, I had hoped it would come as it did, for there was about its eventuation a symbolic rightness and roundness that even to my unsuperstitious mind augured success. Nansen's *Fram* went up for sale, the ideal ship for my purpose, built with consummate foresight and care to resist the ice by rising to its pressure, besides being historically and sentimentally rich in Polar association; and with its unexpected availability, as if it were the unrecognized linchpin of my design, my contingent problems simultaneously vanished. Money to buy it, hitherto hidden, swiftly appeared. Money to outfit it, and to buy dogs and food and to enlist crew, swiftly followed. Within weeks my readiness to seize the moment had been converted into readiness to sail. My thoroughness was vindicated; and, with an appropriately ironic sermon on the virtues of discipline, I told Wisting so.

We chafed, we shuffled, we awaited the tide . . . and as we did the blow fell that on the instant altered radically the configuration of my design. Word reached us, with the rest of the world, that on his final attempt Peary had at last attained the North Pole. His route and his method differed fundamentally from mine, and logic cast at least the shadow of doubt upon the validity of his crucial ultimate measurement; but that, with Cook challenging, would take years to settle, years of controversy, acrimony and inevitable confusion, and meanwhile the laurel of primacy, which I had hoped to win for myself, lay rightly, if perhaps impermanently, with him. The heart of my plan was thus scattered; thenceforward, let me do what I would—duplicate Nansen's drift, plant the Norse flag incontestably at the Pole, accumulate unique scientific data of unarguable quality —I could no longer be *first*.

A blow indeed, for us all; yet I was ready, remained ready, and so without public acknowledgement of the change Peary's feat must make in my own plans we sailed as scheduled, following the route we had charted. As we moved slowly down the Atlantic, however—for we proposed to reach the Bering Strait, where our drift

was to begin, by way of Cape Horn—an alternate idea
took gradual shape in my mind; and as it crystallized,
as amongst us we weighed its prospects and possibilities,
I wondered if perhaps it had not been there all along, an
option against contingency, a cushion against disappointment. For I had, we now agreed, left nothing even to the
chance of Peary's success; and at Madeira I cabled Scott,
by then in Melbourne readying his assault on Antarctica,
my decision: "*. . . going south.*"

Whimsy? Bravado? Call it sportsmanship, that cable,
my try at playing the game the English way; for—
though I acknowledge no man's inherent *right* to be
first, at the South Pole or elsewhere—I recalled only too
vividly Scott's unconcealed rage, a year or two earlier,
when Shackleton, once his subordinate, made his own
attempt; and by putting him on notice that I was entering the race, I proposed to forestall such subsequent
criticism as might charge I had won unfairly, by deceit.
. . . Oh, the English, the English, and their childish
claims of *priority*. As if the Antarctic *belongs* to anyone!

Or perhaps, like Cortez, I was only burning my boats
behind me. From the gesture of my cable, sporting or
cynical, there could be no retreat. I was committed, win
or lose. . . .

My logic, at any rate, was unassailable, and we
steamed south in full confidence of both our preparations and their applicability to our altered design. The
*Fram* was equal to the ice at either latitude. Our dogs
knew no difference between the extremities of either

Pole. Our food, clothing and kit were appropriate, insofar as any could know, to sledging and survival in the geographic and geologic conditions of either climate. Thus much was obvious. Of immensely greater importance, however, was the intellectual preparation I had made, and of which I could assure my companions, for work in Antarctica. Though planning for the North Pole, I had never lost sight of the South. I knew the chart. I knew the coast. I had been there, wintered there. And from them all, the study, the experience, the thought, the imagining. I had developed, albeit without conscious forethought, a *plan*.

The English will view it as a snap decision, no doubt, and an opportunistic one at that, fueled by what in their envy they regard as my ruthless ambition and triggered by Peary's success; but often what seems the impulse of the moment is in fact only the final, visible link in a chain of reasoning welded over so long a time its beginning is lost to conscious memory; or so, at least, it was with my resolution to attempt the South Pole. The completeness of my planning had placed in my hands the means, the knowledge and the will to try the thing; Peary's triumph had fused them. Perhaps the possibility was always there; until the moment came—let them believe me the perfidious thief of Scott's rightful prize though they will—I never recognized it.

It came complete, at any rate, the whole and all its parts, and by the time we reached South Georgia I had determined where we must make our base and how, from it, we should in turn launch our assault. Here my logic, though its origins lay in years of study and thought, became conscious and explicit. If we were to forestall Scott at the Pole, I argued, we must start from a point closer to it. His program called for location of his base camp on or adjacent to Ross Island, a land mass that guaranteed his party a secure footing from which to initiate both its scientific work and its leader's eventual assault on the Pole proper. It was a sound enough plan, conservative and for long-term residence relatively safe; but mine was better. For while Scott's base would be geologically stable, it lay more than eight hundred statute miles from the Pole. My plan proposed a heresy —that we site ourselves on the ice barrier at the Bay of Whales, where, though conventional oceanography held the ice might shift beneath us, we would be sixty miles —a full degree of latitude—further south.

This was not as foolhardy as I suppose it will be made to seem. I had assessed the evidence thoroughly and discovered—despite the prevailing wisdom that the barrier surface is the summit of an immense glacier from which, as any sailor including myself could corroborate, icebergs from time to time break away to drift into the sea —that in fact no slippage had occurred around the Bay of Whales throughout the sixty-eight years of recorded observation; and this anomaly led me in turn to the perfectly sensible conclusion that, at least there, the glacier must rest on a deep footing of rock, the rock in all likelihood of some great and immovable subaqueous island.

In the event our instruments confirmed my proposition, though if hereafter the world chooses to hail the courage of my decision I shall accept—for I shall need—its plaudits; the truth is I took no risk whatever.

Nor were its safety and closer proximity to the Pole the only advantages the Bay afforded. My earlier experience wintering in Antarctica had convinced me that the peculiarities of its air currents make for far milder weather on ice than on land, where winter gales of ferocious intensity are commoner and much steadier; during the period of preparation for our final Polar assault, I reasoned, we should need not only the favor of good weather but, equally important if we were to succeed, the good spirits good weather encourages—when the brief sledging season opened we must be mentally as as well as physically ready. Moreover, its final benefit, the Bay offered the probability of a direct route to the Pole, whereas the path up the Beardmore Glacier I concluded Scott must pursue from his camp at McMurdo Sound would be crooked, difficult and inevitably exhausting; and the outcome obviously has vindicated me in this judgment as well. So much for my foolhardiness.

Framheim: thus I christened our little base upon the ice; and within four weeks of our arrival at it we had completed the work of disembarking our supplies and constructing our quarters. Since no more than a month of the brief Polar autumn remained before the onset of the long winter night, I determined to waste no time on such peripheral occupations as domestic luxury or abstract scientific curiosity. The race between Scott and me must go now to him whose preparations readied him for the final assault at the earliest possible moment the following spring. Our hut was snug, secure, comfortable and warm, our dogs were kenneled, and our provisions were measured and stacked. I gave my companions a day's rest, then issued the order to set our program in motion. Next morning four of us, with three sledges and eighteen dogs, set off south.

Our initial steps were simple but exacting. By my reckoning Framheim lay some seven hundred miles from the Pole. I proposed we establish supply bases a latitudinal degree apart, which is to say at sixty-mile intervals, as far southward as we could travel before the autumn closed. At each we should deposit such quantities of fuel and foodstuffs, for ourselves and the dogs, as I calculated we should require for the final dash; and my calculations were as deliberate and as precise as the calibrations of a fine watch. They rested, of course, on the dogs.

*The dogs are the difference*—as Nansen knew, as I knew, as poor Scott by now must know. . . .

Before we could put that postulate to its ultimate vindication, however, we had first to prepare the route they—and we alongside—should follow next spring. Four days' sledging in a direct line to the Pole brought us without incident to the point at which our sextants confirmed we had reached eighty degrees south. There we laid down our initial supply dump, mounding snow

around and above the provisions we were leaving behind
into an immense cairn and topping the cairn with a long
bamboo pole surmounted by a flag; then—an extra pre-
caution against the possibility of our missing the cairn
later on—we drew an imaginary line east and west
through it and, at intervals of nine hundred yards, set
out flags for five miles in either direction, marking each
with a designation of its distance and placement left or
right from the depot proper. Should the poor visibility
of a blizzard cause us to wander off course on our return,
I have no doubt they will save us essential time in finding our food.

We regained Framheim in two days, our sledges now
almost empty but accordingly lighter, and after a brief
rest set off south again, this time with a party of eight
men plus myself, seven sledges and forty-two dogs.
Four days brought us back to our first depot, which we
found in good condition, and another five to eighty-one
degrees south, where we repeated the procedure, stowing
twelve hundred pounds of food and laying out east-west
markers as before. A day later I sent three men and four
sledges back to base, continuing with the remaining five
a further degree south, there to establish what I now
recognized must be the last depot we should have time
to get down before the onset of winter. Then as we
returned we created a final protection against the possible risks of the coming Polar dash, planting the length
of the route from eighty-two degrees to Framheim with
beacon flags so spaced as to insure unambiguous visibility

from one to the next. Thus again my provision against chance: an hour's forethought at the start might mean a day's gain at the close. So it has and so it will.

Now our preparations moved inside. Three tons of supplies lay ready for us at regular intervals along two hundred of the seven hundred miles to the Pole, but six and perhaps as many as seven months must pass before we could use them. I determined to employ the length and enforced seclusion of our wait to our advantage. Our experience laying depots had familiarized us with the working characteristics of our equipment; I proposed we identify and remedy its defects as well. Though satisfied of the essential practicality of our program, I argued, and my companions agreed, that we could refine it for the further efficiency and safety of our ultimate effort; and this we did, examining every feature of every item, sharing the smallest details of each man's experience, forging from them, with much discussion and some debate, a synthesis toward which our collective good sense seemed to point. One purpose of my stratagem I kept to myself: by occupying my companions' minds exclusively with the goal of our labors I hoped to bring them out of the dangerous prison of winter as keen of morale as they had been on entering it.

At any rate much needed to be done. Our experience confirmed Nansen's view that we should vastly increase our speed and daily mileage if we lightened our loads to the barest necessary minimum. We bent every effort to that end. Stubberud drew the task of unpacking the sledge cases, planing them down and reassembling them on new lines, while Bjaaland, his shop a cubicle cut from the wall of ice behind our hut, rebuilt the sledges themselves, with the help of Hanssen and Wisting, eventually reducing the weight of each from a hundred and sixty-five pounds to forty-eight with no resulting loss of strength. Wisting tore apart our four three-man tents and resewed them into two, and afterward, in light of our discussions, made new lightweight stockings and fresh light flannel underclothing for us all. Hassel designed whip lashes that imitated those used by Eskimos, Stubberud's craftsmanship produced flexible whip handles, and Hanssen bound them together to form fourteen original dog whips, two for each driver. Each of us rebuilt his own ski bindings with an eye toward reconciling utility and lightness. Johansen refashioned our tent pegs to make them lighter and stronger. But we did more than strip our kit. We all joined in inspecting the dog harness, checking every length and joint against hidden weakness and remaking such parts as our tests showed required it. And—in addition to supervising the rest and spending unnumbered hours at mathematical calculation—I myself reworked the dogs, reorganizing the teams, training them back to the feisty edge our depot journeys revealed they had lost on the long voyage from Norway, disciplining them as rigidly as I disciplined myself and my companions, but reminding them always of the affection that bound us together; and though I fed them carefully, on seal meat as well as pemmican, I kept them hungry.

They were the crux of my plan, the indispensable element upon whose efficient performance every other contingency was based. I tried to explain that to a party of Scott's men who, cruising the Ross Sea in the *Terra Nova,* chanced upon our base at the Bay of Whales; but though I argued my case in meticulous detail—and indeed, before they left, offered them the gift of half my teams in the sort of sporting gesture I believed they could appreciate—they went away unconvinced, stubbornly determined to stick it out with ponies and motorized sledges and eventual man-hauling; and I knew then, and grieved at the knowledge, that for all its romantic panache Scott's Polar assault was doomed. For in every respect, in pulling power, in adaptability to the Antarctic cold, in skill on the ice, in their ability to live off the land, dogs held the edge. Nor, persuasive as they were, did my calculations end there. I had weighed everything, every man, every dog, every garment, every sledge, every ounce of food, every pound of equipment, and from the totals struck a balance, between them, the dogs' strength and the distance ahead; then drawn my final figures—the precise point and moment when, as we consumed our rations and the sledges grew lighter, each dog's value as motive power ended and its value as provender began.

*Butcher:* well, they will call me that and worse, I have no doubt. Every humane society from Tasmania to Archangel will seize upon my systematic slaughter of the dogs as proof of my vicious indifference to the costs of my accomplishment and, bestowing on my head the fruits of that bizarre hypocrisy that finds nobility in pets but denies it to their masters, will damn, denounce and ultimately discredit me for my ruthlessness and realism; and the English, their imperious pride stung at losing a prize they consider rightly theirs, will lead the chorus. *Let them.* I too can be sentimental about an animal, I too can cherish a pet, but I saw and I see no difference between a diet built on the slaughter of cattle, swine, sheep and fowl and my diet of dog; and where the Yorkshireman carves his saddle of mutton as much for pleasure as nourishment, I at least killed my dogs to *survive.* . . . Besides, as we discovered, they make a delicious cutlet, with a broth that would gratify the palate of the most fastidious gourmet.

So the winter went, and we worked; and the spring came, and we were ready; and on October 20, 1911, we —myself and four companions, fifty-two dogs and four sledges—set out for the Pole; and—

But there is no "and," no "then," no "whereupon." We simply *went,* our calculations and preparations so exact and so correct that our journey developed as I had foreseen and planned it. The weather favored us. The beacons guided our way. Our rations decreased according to schedule, and as our sledge loads fell, we slaughtered and ate the dogs. We proceeded—though the world and my lecture audiences will wish it otherwise—without misadventure, indeed without adventure of any kind. It was as if—

It was as if I had designed and constructed an elaborate machine that, once set in motion, ran itself.

An anticlimax, surely, but the theme and moral of my life.

Whereupon—well, *one* "whereupon." . . . Whereupon, on December 14, 1911, three days ago, my instruments confirmed we had arrived. *Ninety degrees.* No east. No west. No further measure south. My watch said we were two hours late.

Scott will be later still. . . .

It can never be done again, not like this. The future belongs to younger men, men in aircraft, men with motors. It holds no place for men like me, like—

Like Scott.

. . . And now they stir, stomp their feet, check their straps, check their skis; *time to go.* Go where? Back to Framheim, back to Norway, back to civilization. Back to fame, back to wealth, back to controversy, notoriety, sickness, age, retirement. I do not want that. I do not want to go. I want to *do* again: want to plan, to prepare, to accomplish, want to—

I want to die on the ice.

# SCOTT

## 1912

I SHALL BE THE LAST TO DIE. Wilson went yesterday, or perhaps the day before, having held on to life, to me, to Scott, for as long as he could; but cold and starvation have won after all and now, long drawn face peaceful at last, he lies covered chin to toe by his sleeping bag, like a saint in a shroud, which in fact, in a way, he is. Bowers lies beyond him, great Viking's nose poking the sky, defiant even in death. Of Oates I can think nothing yet beyond awe at the majesty of his sacrifice; and Evans, of course, strong Evans, the strongest of us all, died, who can remember how many weeks past, on the Beardmore Glacier. So now I am alone, will die alone, as I wished, would always have wished, for it has been my duty to see the others through, if not to safety then with what comfort I could give to the deaths all have therefore had to face. Yet it is terrible to die alone. One dreams so, in the end, in the snow, and sometimes one dreams not of the end but of the snow.

Outside the blizzard blows on, an unrelenting shriek, and here and there, though I can detect no opening through which it might have leaked, snow flutters about the tent, forming drifts and cones where it finds a place to rest and gather. Food and fuel lie eleven miles ahead, I know, at One Ton Depot, but I shall never make it now. The weather has seen to that, unseasonable even for Antarctica, so the last of my calculations has proved mistaken too. For myself it makes no matter. Amundsen has beat us to the Pole, beat *me;* but I hate bitterly my failure to get the others through. Yet if I have to die, snow is easy. Even the pain has vanished, the pain of scurvy and frostbite and the gnaw of an empty gut, and only a sort of endless billowing dreaminess remains. I clutch my pencil and write: *I do not think we can hope for any better things now.* The journal, at least, is real.

Snow; snow and Scott, together forever. Scott, Robert Scott, Captain Robert Falcon Scott, though none but Wilson dares risk the liberty of calling me "Scottie," and Wilson only rarely, let alone "Con," as Kathleen does. But then I am that sort of man, that sort of captain, for if it has been my duty to see them through, it has also been my duty to give them faith that I could, faith that I possess, as if by some nearly Biblical blessing, the strength to which they could cling. Yet knowing myself as I do, I know only too well how like other men I truly am; how subject to the doubts and fears and sudden midnight terrors all man feel. No man is God; none is omnipotent nor stronger than the inevitable frailties of flesh and spirit. Yet some few must act as if they are if the rest are to survive at all; some, no matter what, must fabricate the illusion of a godlike strength to which the rest, in pain and dread at their own inescapable weakness, can repair. And such, it seems, has been my lot.

There is that, that vanity; and from it, I suppose, my countrymen will someday make a legend, and from the legend a myth—a bit of Sidney, a touch of Nelson, the Dauntless Commander, the Valiant Explorer, snow solidifying to marble. A special English strain it is, this love of gentle, fallible heroes who somehow lose all winning all, and to my English eyes an endearing one. Yet I can smile at the irony too, for I never longed to be a hero. For that matter I never longed to be an explorer.

As a boy I was small and slight, sickly, poor at games, so easily moved to tears or rage that simply coping with the offhand brutalities of English country life, with its apparent indifference to nature's cruelty, seemed end enough in itself; and if I longed for anything, it was only to grow strong enough to endure the sight of blood, the word or phrase that cut or excluded, the glance that hurt. I *loved* so, my father and mother, my sisters, my friends, my dogs, my pony, even nature in all its malignity; and the least hint that others' love for me might be more casual or conditional than mine for them could cast me into unfathomable darkness. Well, I am that way still, will die that way, but I learned, by training my body till it ached, by dreaming my mind into the selfless captaincies of Arthur and Alfred and Harold the Saxon, to govern my face, my words, my actions, the movements of my limbs. It was a high price to pay, this concealment of the vulnerability within, but I found I had no choice; for to lead others, I knew, I had first to lead myself. To lead has been my fate. Only to Kathleen have I let myself reveal the doubt that cramped my very bowels.

*Fate.* How silly, how sentimental; yet with the dreamy prescience that has always been a part of me, I know that only fate could have brought me into the Royal Navy, brought me Kathleen, brought me here. "Old Mooney," they called me as a cadet, my abstraction and absent-mindedness then as now so conspicuous as to set me off from the raucous, obstreperous vitality of my mates. Yet Barrie, who understands such things, told me, "You are a strange mixture of the dreamy and the practical—never more practical than immediately after you've been dreamy." No doubt Barrie knows also why I could not be happy being ordinary. Myself, I know nothing, except that I am here; *here*—but where is "here"?

As the snow drifts about the tent pole, for so long I drifted, into the Navy, up the ladder of promotion, here and there about the world, lost in a dream so misty I could not have said of what it was . . . into exploration. Picked for the Navy as a boy, I accepted the role of jolly tar as I accepted everything, longing, so far as I could tell, for nothing else; and did well at it too, did the best I could, for I had no capacity for indifference. Then my father died, too soon, too young, and the care of my mother and sisters became my lot as well. Shabby suits, frayed linen, frugal diet: I have known them all and am grateful I have, for from them I learned something more—how to do without. But it was a lonely life.

Old Markham saved me—Sir Clements Markham, whose determination to find what the immense enigma of Antarctica concealed was a dream vast enough to match my own, though, unlike mine, immediate, concrete, detailed. Markham picked me from an entire generation of competent officers, picked me to command the *Discovery* and lead it through and beyond the farthest reaches touched by Cook and Bellinghausen and the Rosses, able fellows all, brave fellows, but hampered by the meagre equipment and skimpier science of their times. It was a vessel into which I could pour all the strength and energy and efficiency I had acquired, an outlet, a focus, at last, for my shifting, drifting dreams; and I took it willingly, engaged finally to the limit of my imagination. And at that too I succeeded—for, with that strain in me that family tradition claims as Scots, I could not help wanting whatever "success" is—and we came home heroes, I and my men, the first to explore and map the Ross Sea, the discoverers of King Edward VII Land, surveyors of McMurdo Sound and Mount Erebus and Mount Terror, collectors of more scientific data about the rocks and fossils and fish and birds and winds and waters and ice and snow of Antarctica than anyone before. But we missed the Pole.

The shapes that people my dreams, sleeping or waking, have always been amorphous and intangible, but the Pole is a phantom so immemorially mysterious that for centuries its merest mention could cause the eyes of seamen everywhere to flare; a goal so inaccessible that captains otherwise sound of judgment plunged to depths of unexcelled grotesquerie in their desperation to imagine it; beyond those impassable ice packs, they sometimes said, must lie an immensity of land so vast as to shrink all other continents to the tininess of Britain herself, while at its heart, though beyond the reach of mortal striving, by extension must lie a place inhabited by indescribably strange creatures: birds and beasts of a color and complexity existing nowhere else, people, if people they could be called, of an intelligence and competence and sensitivity to put the fumbling waywardness of ordinary men to shame; and somewhere there, at the center of so fantastic a world, on a mountaintop perhaps, a mountain of a symmetrical perfection to make all other mountains groveling molehills, lay the Pole. . . . Nonsense, nonsense, I know, the stuff of whisky and spoiled food and solitude too long protracted, nonsense ages since put to rest by the sightings and soundings and measurements of explorers grounded in empiricism; but I caught it too, that fever in the brain, that need to be first to find it. And that first time south, though we told each other we sought only science, I and Wilson and Shackleton tried. God knows how hard we tried. And yet . . .

And yet.

We failed.

But then, science was our goal, too, and science, if not triumph, was served, however hard failure went down; and in the glory of our heroes' welcome home, the decorations, the Audience, the bloody beautiful new suit—the best I'd ever let myself buy—I was able for a time to put failure in its proper place. Whereupon—my shallow breath seems sometimes about to ebb away altogether, but at the thought of her I can feel it come in again with a pang that hurts—whereupon there was Kathleen.

My fingers, nearly numb now, so tighten on my pencil I almost break it, but write: *For my own sake I do not regret this journey.* Write: *I wasn't a very good husband, but I hope I shall be a good memory.* Write, shuddering: *You know I cherish no sentimental rubbish about remarriage. When the right man comes to help you in life, you ought to be your happy self again.* Then for an instant let go and write: *You must know that quite the worst aspect of this situation is the thought that I shall not see you again.* Yet how unkind it is, at the end, to burden her long life to come with my wintry lost love.

For Kathleen is summer, the golden summer of the England I love so and have seen so little, the England of Spenser and Wordsworth, of endless green meadows twinkling yellow with buttercups, trees shadowed but firm in the distance, mists rising above the pools at sunrise, clouds puffy in the sweet blue sky above, dog barking somewhere, fire glowing in the grate; and to smother that loveliness with regret for my inescapable sadness at failure, and the realization that we will never again be together, be one, is to deal the ultimate hurt. But I cannot make myself erase the words. One last time I have to tell her, if only I can, how dearly I love her.

I'd loved before, to be sure, my family, deeply but differently, a pretty girl or two, but never up to the point where dream and reality merged or conflicted; and in fact I knew nothing of love, knew nothing of women, till, thanks to Mabel Beardsley or Barrie or Beerbohm, I sat opposite her at a luncheon on my return. Later she told me she'd thought me, then, the ugliest man she'd ever put eyes on; and no doubt I was, with my balding head and stiff new suit and ignorance of art and style and what was new and exciting—though my smile, she said too, was "rare," my eyes "unusual." Thereafter, I scarcely knew how, we were together whenever I wasn't afloat; for Kathleen was an artist, a sculptor, Rodin's pupil, and knew everyone and everything I didn't: the painters and actors and writers and dancers who inhabited a world concealed from my nautical eyes till then, old Henry James and Isadora Duncan and Ernest Thesiger and Bernard Shaw, all of them dressed as carelessly and talking as off-handedly as if London society and the bloody Royal Navy didn't exist. My need for mastery and my achievement of it had left me so cautious in my daily life I must have seemed to them, to her, the most ordinary of men, too disciplined, too serious, too purposeful; but, with her instinct for the essence in everything, she found the rebel in me, the bohemian, the artist beneath the officer, perceiving in my dream of the Pole a vision like her own. I loved her world, I took to its ease and beauty with a zest that surprised me, as her friends' acceptance of my own drab ways surprised me; and then, deepening my surprise, we were lovers, Kathleen and I, and in her sweet receiving empathy and warm receiving body, I found at last the part of me I'd thought, in my need to make my way, I'd lost. For a year or more, in London, at sea, I lived in a daze that made Polar aurora mere phenomena. . . . The memory hurts, so I do the best I can with my stiff fingers and write: *We took risks, we knew we took them; things have come out against us, and therefore we have no cause for complaint.*

She resisted marrying me, though, tender always, passionate and giving beyond what I could earlier have imagined; but clinging with such tenacity to the independence she'd won at such cost that finally, at the end of my own emotional resources, I thought my love for her hopeless, doomed, myself doomed with it. Yet, strong as she was and will always be, her flashing resilience was of a different order from my stubborn determination, and she found, after all, she needed the iron of my will as deeply as I needed the more keenly tempered platinum of her integrity. So somehow, I by then forty, she past thirty, putting our doubts of ourselves for once aside, we made it up, made it come even, Kathleen writing me, "You and me. You and me. I've always been just *me* before. Now it's you and me and it's *good*."

And it was, we both found, discovering in one another depths of feeling and understanding neither had been quite willing till then to reveal: her need to be, mine to do; and in that recognition of each other's strengths and weaknesses, prides and shames, we learned to make something theretofore unknown to either, something shared, something new. She caught my vision of the Pole as sharply as I caught her compulsion to re-create, with her imagination and her hands, the reality she saw so much more clearly than I; and through that communion, each was able to give the other what, before, we'd needed, sensed, but never found. Then Peter came, within the year, still a buttery baby with golden curls whom I shall never again see or cuddle or toss above me with a whoop and a holler; and I write: *Make the boy interested in natural history if you can. It is better than games.* Write: *. . . keep him in the air.* Write: *Try and make him believe in God, it is comforting,* though I myself wonder endlessly whether God is or is not, wonder, as I wonder about everything, whether I shall ever believe. Then, then, Antarctica again.

To the Pole again too, if we could, but this time,

thanks once more to old Markham, better staffed, better grounded, better equipped; an opportunity, on the grand scale, to study Antarctica as no one had been able to study it before, not even myself and my companions first chance out. And with such a staff and crew as my largest hopes could hardly have envisioned—Wilson and Wright and Debenham and Cherry-Garrard and the invincible Bowers, Evans and Day, Lashly and Campbell and Ponting, that curious northman the ski instructor Gran, and the rest—young, skillful, learned, eager, picked by me from hundreds of volunteers, each for his ability to fit in with the others, to contribute to the effort as a whole, to make the thing succeed. For nearly all of that first year we worked hard out of our base camp at Cape Evans, laying with meticulous care the foundation for our ultimate assault on the Pole, collecting, examining, measuring, recording, discussing, arguing, challenging, revising our ideas, refining our knowledge as it broadened and deepened: food care, frostbite, how the horses and dogs performed, how to dress, how to eat, how to sleep. While I, learning with them, learned also what I alone must know: which to take with me on that final, fateful plunge into the void.

Though I concealed my doubts from everyone but Kathleen, sometimes in the darkness and the cold I'd burst awake, heart pounding, in my fear of the prospect before us: my fear, alike, of the gravity of the risk and the possibility that I might fail to meet it courageously. Morning after morning I went on, though, dogged and

determined, disciplined by commitment and habit and
method and the fact that so many others depended upon
my strength, even if, like all strong people, I wondered
from moment to moment whether, in the end, I should
prove to have as much of it as I, and they, needed. Indeed, my death imminent and inevitable, I still wonder.
Perhaps the journal, gripped between my frozen fingers
like a testament, is a trap by which my weakness may yet
be captured and exposed. I don't know, can't guess. I am
too tired to guess.

A greater shock was to come, however. The *Terra
Nova,* cruising the Ross Sea, discovered Amundsen's
*Fram,* and Amundsen himself, camped on the Bay of
Whales and making no secret, though they said he was
jovial enough about it, of his intention to attack the
Pole in the same relentless, single-minded way he'd gone
after, and found, the Northwest Passage a few years
earlier—which to me meant nothing less than a raiding
party. No mooney nonsense about geology or parasitol-
ogy, no pretext of scientific exploration. I shuddered at
that, and not from the cold either, for Amundsen was—
and, I know now, still is—as intrepid and as tough as a
Viking, accustomed· and acclimated to primitive conditions and unafraid of them or of what he had to do to
cope with them. The news that his crew consisted
mostly of dogs, perhaps as many as a hundred or more,
only underscored it. For I knew then how Amundsen
would make his try: he'd dog-haul his sledges going out,
slaughter the dogs as he neared the Pole and his load

lightened, live off their buried, frozen carcasses coming
back. Well, I myself could never do that. No Englishman could. Even now, dying, gut empty, I can taste a
brackish flavor at the thought. A dog is a friend.

Amundsen must be, after all, a decent sort, a brave
explorer, in many respects a man like myself, if no
Englishman. Yet I did what I had to do, I stuck to my
plan, knowing perfectly well Amundsen might and
probably would be off for the Pole before me, yet convinced, despite awful premonitions, that science must be
served to the end. Wrote then: *The proper, as well as the
wiser, course for us is to proceed exactly as though this
had not happened. To go forward and do our best for the
honour of the country without fear or panic.*

It was the first of November, then, before we set out,
too late, too late. And almost from the start there were
difficulties. The motorized sledges, by which I'd set such
store and from which I'd hoped for so much, proved
worthless. The horses, despite Oates's miraculous minis-
trations, faltered and fell. We'd brought too few dogs
and handled them poorly. The weather had an unseasonable edge, gray and cutting and with temperatures too
low too soon, when in fact it should have been the very
mildest time of the year. The wind on the Great Ice
Barrier was the worst any of us had ever encountered, so
sharp and unrelieved as to be all but unendurable; and,
men and beasts alike stuck, bogged, we lost a crucial
week waiting for a chance to go forward, decreasing day
by day the food and fuel we'd need later on. And al-

ways, at the back of my mind, perhaps at the backs of the minds of all sixteen of us, lurked the terrible suspicion that Amundsen might by now be ahead. Yet I could not clear my imagination of the Pole; and perhaps, I now see, that obsession, so starkly different from the soft green of England, distorted every judgment I made at that fatal time when what were needed most were clarity and balance. Despite my fear of failure, or maybe because of it, I stirred myself to a heartier show of cheer and confidence than ever, giving encouragement here, a smile of approval there, applauding Wilson's cooking, Bowers's determination to keep up his measurements and records, Oates's soldierly stoicism, Evans's cleverness with gear; and thus I stirred them all, when, it now appears, the wiser course might have been to turn back.

Yet we didn't. I am past blaming myself now, past blame itself, for in the face of a death as lonely as this, at least all trivia vanishes, burned, frozen, blown from the bone. The habit of conscience remains, however, like the habit of command; and, dying, I can do nothing less than accept the responsibility for the decision to go on. I stare at my hand, holding the stub of pencil, and it is so white and puffy it might have been sculpted from snow. Write: *Amputation is the best I can hope for now, but will the trouble spread?* Sigh at that show of weakness and write: *Ill fortune presses, but better may come.* For somehow, from some part of me yet unused, I must summon a final measure of strength and give them that,

that hope, give Kathleen and Peter and the world some standard of courage to hold to in the difficult times to come, even if, as I now feel, the world, apart from the tent, is scarcely more than a dimly remembered fiction. Then, suddenly finding what I need, I make myself think for a moment of Oates and his heroism and am thus able to write: *We all hope to meet the end with a similar spirit.*

So we continued, under my undeviating leadership, Day and Hooper turning back at the end of November, Meares and Dimitri and the dog teams at the end of the Ice Barrier, while those remaining, I and eleven more, made our way up the Beardmore Glacier, nearly seven thousand feet high, the hardest task of the journey, sapping us all, I now see, almost to the point of debility, weakening us immeasurably for the final assault on the Pole, by now three hundred fifty miles away or thereabouts across the Antarctic Plateau. Scurvy was beginning to show itself, frostbite was endemic, the bad weather was worsening; and just before Christmas, at Upper Glacier Depot, I sent back Atkinson, Wright, Cherry-Garrard and Keohane, knowing in my heart I'd already decided, perhaps long since, which handful from those still left I'd take with me to the end, yet postponing until the last possible instant my ultimate judgment.

They took it well too, when it came, those who were to remain as well as those who'd return, trusting me, despite aggravated or distressed pride, to have done the right thing; and the leave-taking, gruff and laconic on the surface in the staunchest English way, deeply emotional beneath, went handsomely. In that respect, if no other, I'd led them well. So I and the four Happy Few, the Band of Brothers—Wilson (*the finest character I ever met*), Bowers (*a positive treasure, absolutely trustworthy and prodigiously energetic*), Oates (*a delightfully humorous cheery old pessimist*) and Petty Officer Evans (*a giant worker with a really remarkable headpiece*)—were left to face the Pole, now one hundred seventy miles distant, and whatever it held, while I myself was left to face alone the inevitable but unanswerable question: Had I chosen rightly?

Now, still knowing no answer, knowing I can expect none, I must also ask: Would matters have come out differently had I chosen differently? For that terrible last trek plunged us all into our ultimate selves, testing as nothing else could have done not only our physical resources but, with them, the final measure of our spiritual capacities. Already well past the moment at which, according to our own exacting calculation, chances for success were greatest, we met the bleakest terrain, the harshest and most nearly impassable snow, the coarsest winds, the ugliest falls in temperature any of us could have imagined; and in a burst of self-indulgence I let myself confess to the journal the misery we all five felt: *Great God! this is an awful place.* Committed by my judgment to man-hauling the sledges, committed by agreement to the collection of geological specimens that only increased a load that ought to have been lessening (that I could be certain Amundsen was lessening as exhaustion diminished the strength of his party), we nonetheless by main strength went on and on, daily mileage falling increasingly below what we must make to beat the weather, yet for all my failures, cheered on by my spirit and Wilson's sometimes preposterous cooking, Bowers's resourcefulness, Oates's doggedness, Evans's muscle and brain, nearing the time when, however clearly we'd come to realize we well might fail, we must make the Pole, and maybe miss being first to do so.

Yet no foreboding, however melancholy, could have readied me for the disappointment when it came, too weak a word perhaps, for to my journal at that instant I burst forth: *The worst has happened.* Tragedy, then, for me and my companions, though by the same paradoxical measure Amundsen's triumph, too. No more than a dozen miles from the Pole, as best as by then we could reckon, Bowers's sharp eye picked up way ahead a dark speck that he, that we all, at first believed must be a shadow along the snow, a curl of sastrugi, a trick of the light, but which, as foot after foot between us fell away, we had at last to admit, tears freezing along our eyelids and cheeks, could be nothing less than a cairn, a deliberately moulded mound of snow, topped by a flag, a black flag. Wrote then: *All the day dreams must go.*

What can a man do when the dream is gone? Amundsen's black flag—nothing less, nothing other—and then as the gray day darkened, the signs of Amundsen's priority continued to mount: dog tracks, ski tracks, sledge tracks, footprints, all of them leading, as my own instruments were leading, toward the Pole; which next day, dreaming no longer, not even of it, we reached. Amundsen had pitched his tent there, a tidy affair supported by a single bamboo, Norse flag above, skis upstanding alongside, sextants and spare supplies inside, leaving a courteously deferential note asking me, should I survive instead of himself, to pass on a second note, attached, to King Haakon . . . which I shall, if I can, if I live. Yet no shimmering tower of a mountain rose at the Pole, as the dreams of sailors told, only—

Only Amundsen's black flag. For though it was the Norse flag that flew at the Pole itself it is the black flag that has fluttered down my nightmares since.

Nothing seems simpler than strength once it has been summoned and shown; but at that moment, face-to-face at last not only with the Pole but with the inescapable evidence of Amundsen's priority in attaining it, the despair I'd fought away so long, and thought so long I'd conquered, came rushing back upon me with a fury as feckless as the wind flapping Amundsen's flag. From boyhood on, the Chaos of my imagination and the Order of my will had struggled for possession of my soul; and if in my determination to master, I'd disciplined myself to an Order too rigid, now Chaos in all its formless, aimless horror returned, and it was only a pre-

tense of cheer and sportsmanship and courage with
which I turned toward the haggard, fallen faces of my
companions and, with smiles and gestures and words
that mocked my emptiness, demanded their spirit. But it
worked, and not only with them; for by feigning Order,
I began again to feel its reluctant return. Though I knew
Chaos would now track us to the end, wherever it lay,
it at least slipped back. So we spent the rest of the day
sighting and measuring, allowing ourselves only an instant's rest for a bit of food and a cigarette, our last,
saved for the Pole; and then, at my urging too, we
placed the camera on its tripod, lined up before it, myself standing in the center, Oates and Evans on either
side, Bowers and Wilson seated in the snow before us,
stoutly planted Union Jack behind, and, Bowers pulling
the cable, took our own, as now I know our final, picture. Someday, I suppose, if our bodies are found, the
negative will be developed, the photograph printed. I
hope it will not show the depth of our defeat. I asked
them to smile.

Will it show we knew ourselves doomed? For though
the likelihood of our dying was at that moment a
thought still unspoken, to my journal, to myself, I ad-
mitted my apprehension: *Now for the run home and
a desperate struggle. I wonder if we can do it.* As, a day
or two later: *I'm afraid we are in for a bad pull.* And, a
day after that: *Things beginning to look a little serious.*
It would be, as all of us knew, an eight-hundred-mile
job of it, sledge-hauling the entire way, temperatures

falling rapidly, winds rising, snow surface at its most unpredictably dangerous, and without—what we'd had most of the way out—the support of a party larger than five tired men who'd just stared into the refuse of their own shattered dreams. *I don't like the look of it.* Evans and Oates were suffering from spreading frostbite, Wilson from snow blindness; and though Bowers continued strong and energetic and I was myself, despite my seniority in age, unaware of serious physical decline, I saw what lay ahead for us both in the faces of our three weakening companions. Still—food dwindling and mysteriously short at the depots, fuel running low as our pace fell—we went on, I scarcely knew how, often lagging behind the mileage I'd calculated we must make to beat the winter. But then, approaching the descent of the Glacier, Evans and I fell into crevasses, Evans's second such spill; and afterward, though to that point the strongest of us all, Evans grew increasingly dull and confused, his cuts and wounds suppurating, eyes glazed, needing more and more the help that till then he'd been able to give the rest. *In a very critical situation.* We got him down the Glacier, but by then he could no longer assist at night with the tent (*nearly broken down in brain, I think*); Wilson thought it concussion. But at last, hanging back farther and farther, the poor sick fellow collapsed altogether (*on his knees with clothing disarranged, hands uncovered and frostbitten, and a wild look in his eyes*). Then, we others helplessly watching, he fell into a coma and died.

The first to go, as I myself shall be the last. So at length, now down to four, and Oates noticeably failing, we set forth again, following our own tracks when we could find them, taking bearings and sighting always, weather continuing to worsen. But at the depot we'd laid below the Glacier, we were able to dig out a better supply of horsemeat than we'd let ourselves hope for, which helped a bit to restore our spirits; and, though none of us seemed to sleep well or long, for a day or two it appeared to me we'd regained a measure of the strength we'd lost. Then that too seemed to ebb. The wind kept rising; the surface became more and more difficult (*like pulling over desert sand*), and despite Bowers's ingenuity in rigging the sledges with mast and sail, nothing seemed effective in lessening the exhausting labor of hauling them. Wishing I could feel otherwise, to my journal I confessed the renewal of my doubt: *The rapid closing of the season is ominous. . . . I wonder what is in store for us.*

Well, worse was; temperatures now down to thirty or more below zero; fuel at the depots less and less than we'd expected (*a horrid element of doubt*); food thinning; Wilson in agony from his eyes; all of us frostbitten; daily mileage falling critically: *We are in a very queer street.* Then, stricken at having to do so, Oates showed us his feet.

*Amongst ourselves we are unendingly cheerful,* I wrote, *but what each man feels in his heart I can only guess.* We had no choice, of course, but to urge Oates on,

gangrene notwithstanding, and by insisting he ride one
of the sledges, we perhaps reduced a little the excruciat-
ing pain his toes must have been giving him. But that
meant both a heavier load and one fewer to haul it; and
though Oates went on without complaint, soldier to the
end, his seared face and empty eyes told us everything.
*He has rare pluck and must know that he can never get
through.*

He tried to, though; we all did; and if the rest of us
could see Oates was dying, unable any longer to walk,
taking more and more time in the morning to get into
his boots and thus costing us more and more time on the
march, he did so without explicit complaint, struggling
always to summon some sort of smile to his face. Bravado, to be sure, nothing less than what was to be expected of a captain in the Royal Inniskilling Dragoons.
But then which of us, by that point, was not going on
mostly on bravado of one kind or another? So in fact we
went on, hope dwindling daily, mileage progressively
lessening, winds nearing gale force, snow aswirl with it,
cutting our vision, our faces, deepening the damage to
Wilson's eyes. *Things steadily downhill,* I wrote. *With
great care we might have a dog's chance, but no more.*
But we missed even a dog's chance, gear icing heavily
and more difficult to manage, food short at every depot,
fuel dwindling; though of course I wrote: *I don't know
that anyone is to blame* and meant it, however baffled.
*Cold comfort.*

Yet in the end, moral strength, which we'd all shown,

was not quite enough; for not even Oates's supreme courage could heal the corruption of gangrenous frost-bite. And at last, admitting both his inability to go on and his recognition that his decay was slowing fatally the progress of his companions, the Soldier, as we'd come to call him, begged us either to leave him behind, in his sleeping bag, or give him the means, which Wilson's medical kit after all contained, of ending matters for himself. But we couldn't do that, we *couldn't;* let reason say what it might about the inevitability of Oates's death and, if we stuck with him, our own as well; and knowing what we were saying yet unable to do otherwise, we induced him to try to continue, somehow making a few miles against the blizzard. Whereupon the blizzard rose, making further progress all but impossible, and Oates prayed aloud to die in the night. Yet he didn't, and next morning—now alone, I feel my slowing heart leap again at the memory—next morning the Soldier, after a prolonged battle with his boots, stood suddenly and said, "I am just going outside and may be some time." None of us spoke, though knowing what he intended, and presently, when he failed to return, we staggered into the snow ourselves. But of course he was gone; no trace of him remained. Only the seemingly endless snow remained. Snow will always remain.

I breathe, a shallow breath, but a breath, and write: *We knew it was the act of a brave man and an English gentleman.* Not enough to say, surely, yet what I could say, can say, awed, even upon my own death, by Oates's gallantry. Perhaps the deeper truth is that it has given me and Wilson and Bowers a last standard of humanity to rise to. What greater achievement could Oates have won? One can ask no more.

And indeed there was no more, would be no more. Oh, another desperate day into the wind, and another, a few miles; but by then there was little to choose between the three of us left. Bowers, perhaps, was in the best condition, though badly frostbitten. Wilson was nearly blind, and his hands and feet useless. As for myself, I *like an ass* (I wrote) mixed a small spoonful of curry with my melted pemmican, got violent indigestion, lay awake all night in pain, saw my bad foot turn black. Well, no matter; no doubt by then nothing could have held off the inevitable.

Which now, at last, came. Each day, for days, Wilson and Bowers readied themselves for a final march on One Ton Depot, now only eleven miles ahead. Each day the blizzard stopped them from leaving the tent. And the fuel gave out. And the last of the food went. And the blizzard continued.

And then they died, Wilson and Bowers, quietly, without a murmur of regret, sleeping away in their sleeping bags so slowly that not even I, surviving them, could say with certainty which had gone first; though from the occasional rise and fall of their chests I believed, as I wanted to, that Wilson was last, clinging, noble heart, to life, to me, to Scott, for as long as he could. So finally, except for the howl of the wind, there was only . . . silence.

Silence; yet knowing I must keep my courage high, I

wrote, to the sounds of their expiring breaths: *I do not think we can hope for any better things now. We shall stick it out to the end, but we are getting weaker, of course, and the end cannot be far.*

But that was days ago, I myself scarcely know how many, and in my stiffened hands the journal and the pencil seem almost mute; so I try for a coda and write: *It seems a pity, but I do not think I can write more.* Yet can, after all, and sign my name: *R. Scott.* Then write, pencil falling from my fingers as I end the line: *For God's sake look after our people.*

Are we merely emblems, then? Have we come so far for nothing more than to find so little and die so alone? My mind tumbles with wonder, for if we found no symmetry at the Pole, no shimmering tower of a mountain, in what can I find the symmetry of our lives, our deaths? Surely somewhere the symmetry lies, awaiting my recognition, even if it proves to be nothing more than the symmetry of a snowflake. . . .

Perhaps at that I dozed; perhaps not. One task remains. I raise myself, lean across and close their sleeping bags above the faces of my beloved companions. I have strength for nothing more—except, if it is given me, to *know*.

. . . Snow, then: it will be snow; we are all of us flakes of snow, blown willy-nilly through God's eternal night.

THE DISCOVERY OF THE BODIES of Scott and his comrades in November 1912 brought the tragedy, the triumph and the era to a close; thereafter exploration of Antarctica was based on—and safeguarded by—technology of a sophistication explorers of the heroic period could only dimly foresee. Shackleton's grit, guts and gift for leadership took him on to two further exploits, but as before, he was destined to attempt more than he could attain: his dream of crossing Antarctica from the Weddell to the Ross Sea ended with the loss of the *Endurance* in 1915, and his last assault on Terra Australis was aborted by his death off South Georgia in 1922. Amundsen, whose accomplishments as an explorer are unparalleled—he was first to sail the Northwest Passage, first at the South Pole and probably first at the North Pole as well—vanished over the Arctic in 1928 while trying to save the life of a man who had sought relentlessly to discredit and destroy him. Scott's posthumous fate was equally ironic: his meticulous diaries not only confirmed the thoroughness of his rival's achievement but by their noble stoicism and immaculate language established his place among those durable

English heroes revered as deeply for the beauty of their failures as for the brilliance of their successes; of him it can truly be said that nothing so became his life as the manner of his losing it.

THIS IS A WORK OF FICTION, not biography, for it attempts to depict and portray what biography may only identify and describe; but its roots are biographical, and though I have imagined and invented freely I have done so within the bounds established by the record. My bibliographical obligations are thus numerous, especially to Amundsen's *My Life as an Explorer* and *The South Pole,* Shackleton's *The Heart of the Antarctic,* the diaries contained in *Scott's Last Expedition,* Cherry-Garrard's *The Worst Journey in the World,* the Fishers' *Shackleton and the Antarctic,* and both of the biographies, Pound's and Seaver's, entitled *Scott of the Antarctic.*

I am also greatly indebted, for material support, to Philippe Labro of Paris, to Washington & Lee University and its John M. Glenn Grants-in-Aid program, to Mr. & Mrs. John J. Jenkins of New Canaan, Connecticut, and to Mr. Oscar van Leer, president, Royal Packaging Industries van Leer B.V., of Amsterdam; and, for the generous use of its incomparable library and archives, to the Scott Polar Research Institute of Cambridge University.